Body,
Paper,
Stage

Qualitative Inquiry and Social Justice

Series Editors

Norman K. Denzin
University of Illinois–Champaign Urbana

Yvonna S. Lincoln
Texas A&M University

Books in this series address the role of critical qualitative research in an era that cries out for emancipatory visions that move people to struggle and resist oppression. Rooted in an ethical framework that is based on human rights and social justice, the series publishes exemplary studies that advance this transformative paradigm.

Volumes in this series:

Betweener Talk: Decolonizing Knowledge Production, Pedagogy, and Praxis
Marcelo Diversi and Cláudio Moreira

Body, Paper, Stage: Writing and Performing Autoethnography
Tami Spry

Body, Paper, Stage

Writing and Performing Autoethnography

Tami Spry

Left
Coast
Press
Inc.

Walnut Creek
California

LEFT COAST PRESS, INC.
1630 North Main Street, #400
Walnut Creek, CA 94596
http://www.LCoastPress.com

ISBN 978-1-59874-486-6 hardcover
ISBN 978-1-59874-487-3 paperback

Library of Congress Cataloging-in-Publication Data
Spry, Tami.
 Body, paper, stage : writing and performing autoethnography / Tami Spry.
  p. cm.— (Qualitative inquiry and social justice)
 Includes bibliographical references and index.
 ISBN 978-1-59874-486-6 (hardcover : alk. paper) — ISBN 978-1-59874-487-3
(pbk. : alk. paper)
 1. Ethnology—Biographical methods. 2. Ethnology—Authorship. 3.
Autobiography. I. Title.
 GN346.6.S67 2011
 305.8—dc22
                    2011006964

Printed in the United States of America

⊚™ The paper used in this publication meets the minimum requirements of
American National Standard for Information Sciences—Permanence of Paper for
Printed Library Materials, ANSI/NISO Z39.48–1992.

Contents

For my lovely mother, Belle,

who told me I was a writer;

and

for my sweet baby boy, Keller,

who helped me write a book about living.

Did I actually reach out my arms
toward it, toward paradise falling, like
the fading of the dearest, wildest hope—
the dark heart of the story that is all
the reason for its telling?

Mary Oliver
"The Chance to Love Everything"

Foreword

Performing Authoethnography: Making the Personal Political

Body, paper, stage, the performative I. We study performances, our bodies are written about, bodies move from page to stage, bodies perform in the presence of others. Experience, performance, words: these are the places to begin. Personal experience reflects the flow of thoughts and meanings people have in their immediate situations. These experiences can be routine or problematic. When described, they assume the shape of a story, a narrative, as when we put words on a page. These lived experiences can not be studied directly. Rather, they are mediated by language, speech and other systems of mediating discourse. Mediation defines the very experience one attempts to describe. We engage these representations of experience, not the experience itself. We bear witness to the stories people tell one another about the experiences they have had. Self stories are interpretations, made up as the person goes along—performances on the run—their meanings glimpsed sideways in the rearview mirror.

Many now argue that we can study only our own experiences. The researcher merges with the research subject. We can only write from the space of the personal, about our own bodies, feelings, hungers, desires, hopes, dreams, fears. Ethnography becomes a critical performance grounded in the interpretations of the writer. This is the topic of Tami Spry's powerful new book.

Indeed her multi-voiced text is an example of such writing; it performs its own narrative reflexivity. She shows us how to move from the body—our lived performances—to the written page, and from the page to the stage, that uncertain, unstable site where we navigate gender, class, language, race, intimacy, power, and politics. Spry masterfully reviews the arguments for creating personal experience narratives, anchoring her text in the discourses of critical performance studies.

She reviews the history of, and arguments for, this form of writing, the challenge of creating texts from events that unfold in the life of the writer, while embodying tactics that enact a progressive politics of resistance. Such texts, when performed (and writing is a form of performance), enact a politics of possibility. They shape a critical awareness, they disturb the status quo, they probe questions of identity.

Spry writes out of her own history with this method. She shows how performative autoethnography as a critical reflexive methodology provides a framework for making the personal political in the post-September 11 world. She writes and performs from the spaces of hurting, healing, grieving bodies—her own grief at the loss of her son at childbirth, the death of her mother, the bombings of 9/11. She offers a pedagogy of hope, a critical/indigenous ethnography. Her essay is about autoethnography as a radical resistant democratic practice, a political practice intended to create a space for dialogue and debate about issues of injustice. Her book tells by showing: performance fragments, absent histories, embodied possibilities, story-telling, a performative I. Personal biography collides with culture and structure, turning historical discourse back on itself. Her performative I is embodied, liminal, accountable, wild, free, moral.

To enable others to engage in this same discourse, Spry offers guidance for the novice including writing exercises, engaging theoretical questions, and practical suggestions for the writer and performer. She ends with a call for collaborative performances, grounded in the belief that together we can create a local and global respect, that we can love and care for one another.

This is a place to begin.

Norman K. Denzin

Preface

Autoethnography Lost and Found

Autoethnography is body and verse.
It is self and other and one and many.
It is ensemble, acapella, and accompaniment.
Autoethnography is place and space and time.
It is personal, political, and palpable.

It is art and craft. It is jazz and blues.
It is messy, bloody, and unruly.
It is agency, rendition, and dialogue.
It is danger, trouble, and pain.

It is critical, reflexive, performative, and often forgiving.
It is the string theories of pain and privilege
     forever woven into fabrics of power/lessness.

It is skin/flints of melanin and bodies
 in the gendered hues of sanctuary and violence.
It is a subaltern narrative revealing the understory of
 hegemonic systems.
It is skeptical and restorative.
It is an interpreted body of evidence.
It is personally accountable.

It is wholly none of these, but fragments of each.
It is a performance of possibilities.

Acknowledgments

Being a performance studies artist/scholar is a deeply embodied intimate enterprise. We live and breath and do the thing we study. Performance cannot be done alone; it cannot be created or thought of or imagined alone. And so before personal acknowledgements, I must recognize that it is the community of performance studies in all of its artistic and scholarly diversity and richness that continually moves me to write. And without question, the artistic and scholarly DNA of Wallace Bacon and Dwight Conquergood are the corporeal building blocks of *Body, Paper, Stage*.

This book has been a long time coming. Simply put, it could not have been written without the unfailing love and encouragement of my husband, Barry Scanlan. His support, both emotional and logistic, was unconditional. Our son Zeb's somatically artistic languaging of the world remains a constant inspiration personally and professionally. My dear friend and rhetorician Marla Kanengieter is woven into the fabric of this book. Her grace and intellect are unparalleled; throughout our years of conversation she has helped me define and redefine the foundations of language and experience, let alone holding my hand during some very dark years. John Capecci and I have been friends for the better part of our lives; he understands me in ways I do not, and I can't imagine my life or this book without him. Elyse Pineau. You know who you are. The full opening of your voice fills these pages and my life. Though, or maybe because, his PhD is in rhetoric, Dan Wildeson articulates the depth and felt-sensing of performance in ways that break ground both disciplinarily and personally.

My life has been deeply enriched by the friendship and guidance of D. Soyini Madison and Norman Denzin. I have been transformed by their commitment to social/personal/political justice locally and globally. Soyini allows me to understand what it means to breath performance, that the body in performance is the blood, bone, and muscle of knowledge. Norman Denzin's unabashed passion for a critical pedagogy of possibilities in these troubling times has been a deeply reassuring beacon of light. His creation of outlets for person-ally political work for change has been life saving for so many of us. Knowing him is one of the great gifts of my life.

This book also exists because of the deep personal/scholarly influence of Craig Gingrich-Philbrook and Della Pollock who are two of the best hearts and minds of our discipline. The brilliant linguistic love and support of our writing group consisting of Ken Gale, Ronald Pelias, Larry Russell, and Jonathan Wyatt threads the bindings of this book. And to Annette Martin for teaching me the discipline of the stage.

Finally, as mentioned in the first pages, this book is dedicated to my mother Belle Marie Spry and our late son Keller Winfield Spry Scanlan.

Introduction

The Textualizing Body

Bodies of/as Evidence in Autoethnography

The process of performative autoethnography is a bit like a *CSI* episode. It starts with a body, in a place, and in a time. The investigators analyze the body for evidence, the body as evidence, the body of evidence. But evidence, like experience, is not itself knowledge; like evidence, experience means nothing until it is interpreted, until we interpret the body as evidence. For a performative autoethnographer, the critical stance of the performing body constitutes a praxis of evidence and analysis. We offer our performing body as raw data of a critical cultural story. So, when I perform "Presence and Privacy: Ode to the Absent Phallus" (1998), a performative autoethnography of sexual assault, the audience not only sees my body as evidence of an assaulted body, they also see my body performing a reflexive critique upon dominant cultural notions of victim and survivor contextualized in that place and in that time. If autoethnography is epistemic, then the evidence of how we know what we know must reside in the aesthetic crafting of critical reflexion upon the body as evidence.

In postmodern research, we sometimes like to think of the body as inherently "knowing" things without remembering that the body knows what language constructs. The story comes from a critically reflexive location where the autoethnographer seeks to construct a plural sense of self, a dialectic of copresence with others in the field of study concerning how bodies are read in various contexts of culture and power.

Performance, which at its heart is the embodiment of language, has also taught me a skepticism of language's ability to represent me or others outside of the dominant master narratives that it is meant to serve. This skepticism of language's ability to represent the body as evidence motivates the critical reflection upon the systems of power held in place through language. Further, performative autoethnography is critically ethnographic due to its embodied analyses of power in cultural structures and systems. In her book *Critical Ethnography: Methods, Ethics, and Performance*, D. Soyini Madison writes, "The critical ethnographer also takes us beneath surface appearances, disrupts the *status quo*, and unsettles both neutrality and taken-for-granted assumptions by bringing to light underlying and obscure operations of power and control" (5). Performative autoethnography reveals the *understory* of hegemonic systems.

All of this rests upon reading and writing the body as a cultural text, as a personally political reflection whose evidence is an aesthetic/epistemic praxis based in performative writing. The following are a few segments of embodied theorizing that seek to negotiate the tensiveness, the push and pull between the aesthetic and the epistemic that creates the evidence of performative autoethnography. Rather than a coherent whole, the following are glimpses, fragments, understories.

For some time now, my work has focused upon an ethnography of loss and healing. The body is tantamount in this work as it is the presence and absence of bodies that constitute the experiential evidence of loss. A passage from a work on the loss *of our child, "Paper and Skin: Bodies of Loss and Life" (2004):*

The words are unmeshed in the blood and bones of the mother and child. Arms ache and disarm themselves with the visceral absence of the other. Writing doesn't help me put my arms back on, but it does help me to remember that I had arms, and then, to show me that the arms are still usable in a way I can't yet understand.

In trying to make meaning within a culture of absence, I have lost and found and lost again many religions. But the practice I keep coming back to, the meaning-maker that never seems to fail is writing.

For me, prayer has become the aesthetic practice of crafting meaning.

Being in performance studies

has taught me about faith.

At the beginning of rehearsal,

one is always afraid,

vulnerable,

and hoping to believe.

Even, and especially when,

we don't think we will ever make present

what seems so absent.

One of my lost religions is Catholicism. When a Catholic walks up to the priest to take Holy Communion, the mouth opens, the priest holds the wafer to the outstretched tongue and says, "The body and blood of Christ." The tongue says, "Amen", and then he, because he is *always* a he, places the wafer onto the tongue, whereupon you are to swallow the body and blood-in-a-wafer of the Savior. The wafer, however, usually sticks to the roof of the mouth, flesh against flesh, resisting the patriarchal directive to swallow.

Now, I replace wafers with words. Writing is communion. No longer waiting for them to be placed in my mouth by man, words are the body and blood...of life, and of loss. Making the absent present, words reconstruct the body of a lost mother, or father, or son, or Holy Ghost. Writing of his absence helped me find my son, helped me know his presence, and then his stillness, as a gift, as a prayer, as a Hallelujah.

Writing of loss through an aesthetic/epistemic praxis of performative autoethnography has provided me evidence of hope and beauty. I have tomes of writing revealing personal experience and describing emotion, but this writing did not help me find my son, or to know his presence, or move me from loss to hope. Performance studies has been based in the analysis and embodiment of emotion for centuries. We know that knowledge is evocative, and that evocation of emotion is not itself aesthetic or epistemic; artful knowledge is constructed, as Elyse Pineau (2000) might say, through the "articulate body." As we develop "post" methodologies we may be in danger of expecting the personal or emotional to stand in for literary acumen. Performative autoethnography resides in the intersections of knowledge construction and art, in the aesthetic articulation of the performative body, in a recuperation of a life after death.

A passage from "Paper and Skin: Bodies of Loss and Life" (2004):

> I am wreckage. I am free floating, P-Funk, feet-don't-fail-me-now, Electric Bogaloo wreckage. More or less. Ambiguous in all my artificial mediated fracturesque construction, writing is the only ritual I can enact right now. Words the only thing my body can feel. I am the hermit coming in and out of her cave, looking for a sign that she has been in the darkness long enough to heal the wounds that would crack from too much sunlight. I am the warrior goddess siren virgin leading us into battles of passion and righteousness and standing dumbfounded still and scared and weak. More or

less. I am Shirley Temple, Sheila E., John Travolta, John the Baptist, and I wish I were Janice. I wish I could just sing and not care or care too much and feel the drugs and hear the sound of my voice tied to the whipping post as you scream and cheer the raspy edges of my soul coming out my mouth. I am alive and kickin'. I am dead and rotting. I am whoop-ti-do wreckage trying to forget that my body makes language like hair. (25)

It is, as Dwight Conquergood says, a "performance-sensitive way of knowing" (1998, 26) that has walked me through the shadowlands and sat with me in the bottomless pits. Della Pollock (1998)writes saying that performativity "becomes the everyday practice of *doing* what's *done*" (43). Realizing that I was doing grief gave me agency to keep breathing, like Emily Dickinson, "Because I could not stop for Death —/ He kindly stopped for me —/ the Carriage held but just Ourselves —/ And Immortality" (1981, 712). And then the Carriage keeps going. Performatively, Dickinson knew that Death is an everyday practice of breaking and remaking meaning, of colliding and realigning with history.

Writing as prayer, as communion, and writing as redemption. The following is an excerpt from a writing group that I am in:

Caverns

My office is in a beautiful, old, rather dusty and frumpy WPA constructed building. I have a wall of huge old drafty ten foot windows that look out on the trees in the summer, then reveal the Mississippi River in the winter.

Today is gray and rainy and cold. So am I.

Keller, our lost son, would have been five years old this week. And today my insides feel as if it could never sustain life again, and surely, at 47, that will soon be a reality. A graying womb. Cavernous as my office, as the low clouds, as the Mississippi.

But then one of you writes of Rufus Wainwright's version of "Hallelujah," and I am becoming redeemed through the chorus of "Hallelujah" that is this group.

There is, for me, redemption happening in the text of bodies as constructed through our writing. Here, in the midst of performativity, the words are doing redemption. It's not as if I feel like I'm going to be "OK" after the redemption is "over." The loss will always be there, the ghost of his body moving in and out of me; but it is because, as Kenneth Burke (1989) would say, we are "wordlings," "being bodies that learn language," that the loss is not stagnant, rigid. Putting language to his body just...brings him (to) life. "Performativity," write D. Soyini Madison and Judith Hamera (2006a), "becomes all at once a cultural convention, value, and signifier that is inscribed on the body—performed through the body—to mark identities" (xviii). I can make words with him, but making them in collaboration with all of you helps me identify his body differently, helps me make the loss differently, helps me know him differently, and here, find redemption in the making.

Hallelujah.

Beauty

Some years ago, I attended a workshop with Maxine Hong Kingston.

She asked us to make a list of things we were afraid to write about.

That year had brought 9/11,
    a lost child,
    a lost father,
    and a slew of hopes lost with the death of Senator Paul
    Wellstone.
And in the face of our lists,
She asked us to write about beauty.
And I froze.
I realized that in the presence of so much loss,
Beauty was the thing I was most afraid to write about.
Afraid
that I might not find any,
or not know it when I see it,
or not be worthy of it,
or find that I have squandered it,
or that I don't deserve it,
or that I might not be it.

I wish I could say
that following the workshop with this beautiful woman
I have been writing in beauty
and am no longer afraid.

I am
finding moments
of beauty
And have begun to be less afraid
of fear.

In her book *Small Wonder,* Barbara Kingsolver writes, "You can look at all the parts of a terrible thing until you see that they're assemblies of smaller parts, all of which you can name, and some of which you can heal or alter, and finally the terror that seemed unbearable becomes manageable" (xiii). Loss is a fragmentation of terrible things, shards of evidence that we can interpret as grief and hope and beauty. Performative autoethnography is about bodies, in a place, and in a time. The depth of meanings I make of those bodies, present and absent, is directly related to the commitment of embodying the aesthetic as an imperative of this methodology. Pineau's articulate body in "Nursing Mother" (2000) is aesthetic due to its analytic acumen, and epistemic due to its deft embodiment of literary style. Pelias's brilliant "girly-man" (2007) digs into the un/seen spaces of masculinity and privilege because he constructs on the page a living, breathing, devastated, and desiring body for us to touch, to scrutinize.

For me, autoethnography is performative/skeptical/multiple. It is also in the service of simultaneously deconstructing what it might be putting together, which is, for me, the continual process of critical reflexion. It is, definitely, a nervous condition, as Pollock (1998) decries, but, paradoxically, this writing practice is prayer and offers me peace.

Body of the Book

Body, Paper, Stage is about intersections, negotiations, collisions, and coalesces involved in performing critical autoethnography. It is about putting the body on the page, lifting it to the stage, and then understanding that body and paper and stage *are* one another, that there is no purity of text or hierarchy of embodiment. "Bodies of/ as Evidence in Autoethnography" reveals the interrelations of critically reflecting on how our bodies are inherently part of the meaning making process, how the meaning making process is inherently tied to language and writing, and how performance operates as the dialogic process within and between the body and language. "Bodies" illuminates the *doing* of performative autoethnography, or what it is and what it does. Consider another example from "Paper and Skin: Bodies of Loss and Life":

Pieces

I sit left of center stage in a straight-backed wooden chair with no arms. Pieces of paper lie scattered about me, some whole, some torn. From where I sit, I can read some of the pieces. There are words or bits of words, forming a grammar of fear and confusion. Agitated, I rise from the chair. My arms break off my shoulders and bounce stiff and clumsy about my ankles on the stage. I stumble trying to assemble the shards of this language, fractured fairy tales from the wreckage of a birth and death. I lurch within the boundaries of the stage trying to read the pieces, trying to remember sentence structure, trying to piece together an alphabet. (Spry 2004)

In performative autoethnography, words may fall about us; we may sometimes lurch within the boundaries of performance only to stumble upon a shard of language telling the messy beauty of being with others; old grammars of fear may fracture under the weight of oppression leveled upon us—or that we have leveled upon others. The process of writing and performing critical autoethnography, or *performative autoethnography* as it will be conceptualized here, is the continuous negotiation of accounting for who we are with others in culture on page and stage and back again. As such, this book inhabits the intersections of performance studies, critical ethnography, and autoethnography for the purpose of explicating performative autoethnography.

The overall purpose of this book, in relation to the overall disciplinary purpose and goal of performance studies, is to present a method for an *engaged, critical, and embodied pedagogy, in other*

words, learning from and in performative autoethnography. The title
of the book suggests the interdependent process of performative
autoethnography. *Body* refers to 1) its material corporeal make-
up including size, sex, color, etc., and 2) the performativity of the
body, how it is *read* and what it *does* in culture. *Paper* refers to composing autoethnography in how we and others assign words to the
body's sociocultural experience. *Stage* refers to the aesthetic process of creating performance as it is used as a method of inquiry,
as a heuristic tool in enacting autoethnographic analysis on stage.

Thus, *Body, Paper, Stage* has three interdependent purposes:

1. Body: To offer the *performative-I* as a critical heterogeneous
   autoethnographic research disposition constructed through
   the body's continual negotiation of self/other/culture/language.

2. Paper: To offer a conceptualization and methodology of
   composing autoethnography through a critical and embodied *performative-I disposition.*

3. Stage: To offer a conceptualization and methodology of performing autoethnography through a critical and embodied
   performative-I persona.

The Textualizing Body

Though we will present a clear and comprehensive methodology
of composing and performing autoethnography, it is essential to
understand that the methodological processes of analysis, composition, and performance are deemed interdependent through the
concept of a *textualizing body* where no epistemological hierarchy
exists between page, stage, word, or body; the body/self, the autoethnographic text, and the performance of the text contribute equally
to the meaning making process. In performative autoethnography,
performance is not an added scholarly bonus. It does not operate as
an interesting feature or entertaining option that one might choose
after "finishing" the autoethnography. Here, performance does not

"illuminate" the text, rather is assists in the creation of the text; it is in itself performative.

The composition and performance process continually forms and reforms the body, the body of the text, the text of the body. In other words, the literary and the performative collaborate in autoethnographic epistemology. W. B. Worthen (2008) discusses hierarchies in performance based on origination:

> From the 'literary' perspective, the meaning, and so the authority, of performance is a function of how fully it expresses the meanings, gestures, themes located ineffably in the structures of the work, which is taken both as the ground and origin of performance and as the embodiment of authorial intention. (12)

Any new insight into the text through performance, argues Worthen, is seen still as embedded in the literary work with performance as a tool for expressing insight, or as an interpretive "demonstration" of the literature. "Stage vs. page, literature vs. theatre, text vs. performance" writes Worthen, "have less to do with the relationship between writing and enactment [performance] than with power, with the ways we authorize performance," positioning performance as *assisting* epistemology rather than *enacting* epistemology.

In performative autoethnography the textualizing body is a collaboration between body, page, and stage. Here, knowledge is constructed through performance as fully as through composition. Performance is constructive *of* the composition process through performativity, through critical reflection upon the material and socially constructed body of the autoethnographer as performance; the process of performative autoethnography seeks to identify and call into question performances of class, race, gender, and other performativities marked as normative and restrictive by creating alternative ways of being through performance. What is written from the body changes the body and vice-versa; what is performed turns back upon itself, changing word and body. In performative autoethnography, body/performatives, paper/word, and stage/

performance are in flux, in process, in progress as they continually (re)generate one another in a Deleuzian cycle of becoming, none existing as fixed or static, none positioned as authority.

So, although our goal is a solidly crafted well rehearsed auto-ethnographic performance, its construction and pedagogy is based in its interdependency of body, paper, and stage which in turn comprise the organization of this book. Viewing them as structurally and pedagogically interdependent, it is clear by now that body, paper, and stage are metaphors for the three components of performative auto-ethnography. As such, chapter 1, *Body*: Conceptualizing Performative Autoethnography, will present the performative-I as the subjectivity upon which our process is built. The performative-I is the positionality of the researcher in performative autoethnography and is based in a negotiation between self/other/culture/language, a system of relation between body/I/we/word. Through a performative-I disposition, the researcher constructs a story of her critical engagement with others in culture. She "gives an account of [her]self" (Butler 2005) by identifying and critically reflecting upon a particular personal experience intersecting the politics of culture. This performative-I disposition is founded in the ethical check and balance of agency (the empowerment of telling one's story) and representation (the sociocultural responsibility of telling one's story). Chapter 2, *Paper*: Writing the Body, will explain the composition process as built upon an ethic of aesthetics and will discuss what is at stake for us personally and politically in composing autoethnography. Chapter 3, *Paper*: Composing Performative Autoethnography, offers a five part methodology of writing which includes 1) sociocultural context, 2) critical self-reflection, 3) self-other interaction, 4) the body, and 5) ethics. Then, chapter 4, *Stage*: Performing the Autoethnographic Body, will pose the question of who and what we are performing in performative autoethnography. I argue that a persona exists in the autoethnographic text that *is and is not* the autoethnographer. It is a performative-I persona, a particular construction of self, that the autoethnographer seeks to embody through performance. In chapter 5, *Stage*: Embodying Performative

Autoethnography, our performance method, called *the elements of an embodied performance*, extends the composition process into the body on stage.

Through the idea of the textualizing body, these chapters comprise a non-hierarchical and interdependent performative pedagogy; the body, the paper, and the stage rely on one another for imagining and creating possibilities for personal and political transformation. Before moving into chapter 1, we will establish a focused conceptualization of performance and of autoethnography as they are both used in a multiplicity of ways across disciplines.

Studying Performance

Because of its seemingly easy access, performance, with its capabilities as a method of critical and cultural inquiry has enjoyed much attention in contemporary scholarship and practice. However, within this burgeoning and often productive turn toward performance, it is not always evident that the epistemological potentialities of performance are best manifested through rigorous study of the considerable scholarly history and contemporary theory/methodology praxis in performance studies. In *Opening Acts: Performance in/as Communication and Cultural Studies*, Judith Hamera notes that generating a complex understanding of performance "means exchanging the exuberant 'innocence' of 'discovering' performance and claiming it for oneself alone for the rich and diverse intellectual neighborhood of hardworking, precise, and playful interlocutors, whose creative scholarly turns inspire defter, richer ones in those who engage them" (2). And then, even within a rigorous study, the ways and means of performance are vast, multiple, and contested. So a convergent and studied focus of performance allows for a defter and richer scholarship.

Body, Paper, Stage is grounded in the disciplinary convergences of performance and ethnography that "privilege the body as a site of knowing" (Conquergood 1991, 180). Embedded in the performative turn toward ethnography and the ethnographic turn toward performance, the development of performative autoethnography as method, as process and product, our conceptualizations about what it *is* and what it *does* have become deeply generative and heuristic across disciplines. The "crisis of representation" in the social sciences and humanities was not so much a crisis for performance studies artist/scholars as it was a recognition of a familiar (Spry 2006). Our disciplinary roots are grounded in interpretation, a process wrought with the crisis and complexity of representation through performance. The "performative turn" in ethnography (Turner 1986) has served to expand the scope and recognition of the cultural/political implications of performance studies. Similarly, performance studies theories of embodiment and textual interpretation inform ethnographic methods of ethics, researcher positionality, cultural performances, and fieldwork (Conquergood 1985; 1991, Schechner 1985). In 1998, Mary Strine mapped the "cultural turn" in performance studies asserting that the "cultural-performance matrix" 1) resituated literature as "an always politically inflected form," 2) refocused perspectives on how performative forms and practices have served to "produce, sustain, and transform" systems of power and dominance, and 3) directed us toward less traditional texts (personal narratives, oral histories, performance art) (6–7). Strine, with Conquergood, argued that this cultural/performance matrix signals a paradigmatic shift "from performance as a distinctive *act* of culture to performance as an integrated *agency* of culture" (7).

The dialogic engagement between ethnographic studies of performance and performance studies of ethnography continue to expand our knowledge of self/other/context by continually (re) activating our methods of representation. These methods assist in approaching crises as political fissures in the *status quo*, as fractures interrupting hegemonic practices, and as ruptures in imperialistic research routines. Performance and ethnography continually turn back upon themselves emerging as praxes of participatory civic social action (Conquergood 2004; Denzin 2003; Madison 2005; Schechner 1985).

From within this culture/performance matrix, in *Body, Paper, Stage* performance is conceptualized as constitutive of sociocultural realities, as epistemic, and as a method of critique, and operationalized as a critical method of embodiment in the writing and performance of autoethnography. "Performance creates," writes Elisabeth Bell (2008), "performance is a way of knowing, and performance is a way of staking claims about that creation or knowledge" (18). How and what "performance creates" will be further distinguished in chapters 4 and 5.

Overall, we undertake performance as a radicalizing process of knowing. It is radicalizing in its approach to learning as embodiment, or as learning through the body. We know who we are by reflecting upon how we choose to communicate with others, or how we perform ourselves in our everyday life. Performative autoethnography is the assigning of language to those critically reflected upon experiences.

Studying Autoethnography

Quoted earlier, the excerpt "Pieces" is the opening of a larger work of mine that seeks to tug at some of the inchoate strands of personal and political loss and grief and hope. The images of fear and fragmentation, of wreckage and language in "Pieces," parallel for me the provocative and (spell)binding state of affairs of autoethnography. With its seductive possibilities in explicating knowledge through represented lived experience, autoethnography has been met with profound interest from both the humanities and the sciences. The extensive use of autoethnography in the fields of education, medicine, performance studies, sociology, communication studies, and many more, speaks to a transdisciplinary desire for methodology that can articulate the intersections of histories, cultures, and societies through the critical representation of a researcher's experience.

In moving away from the positivist notion of the researcher "as a detached head...floating from research site to research site thinking and speaking, while its profane counterpart, the Body, lurks unseen, unruly, and uncontrollable in the shadows of the Great Halls of Academe" (Spry 2001, 720), we having been coming to terms with the fact that the heart, body, mind, spirit et al. have always and already been present in research. In claiming that the emperor of positivism has no clothes, we find a living, breathing body of lived experience. This decloaking, then, has motivated alternate and embodied forms of reporting scholarship such as autoethnography, performance ethnography, personal narrative, sociopoetics, and others (Alexander 2006, Anzuldua 2007, Conquergood 1991, Denzin 2003, Ellis and Bochner 2006, Gingrich-Philbrook 2005, Muncey 2010, Pelias 2004, Pineau 2000, Pollock 199, Richardson and St. Pierre 2005, Spry 2006, Trinh 1989). The last two decades have seen a colossal burgeoning of these alternate forms, so much so that a researcher seeking to employ such forms may find him or herself "trying to assemble the shards of language" (Behar 1997) and methodological approaches.

Many kinds of writing and representation exist under the umbrella of autoethnography. Starting with the "crisis of representation" in the social sciences and humanities, this deliberation on the politics of linguistic representation of cultures began in earnest in the 1980s, articulated by Clifford and Marcus, Conquergood, Fabian, Geertz, Jackson, and others. Self-reflexivity is employed in autoethnography that "breaks your heart" (Behar 1997), and that engages a "methodology of the heart" (Pelias 2005). In a 2009 representative survey of poetic inquiry in the social sciences, Monica Pendergast asserts that poetic inquiry is "a calling between the 'I' and the 'Other,' a call-and-response, a song that is sung, a voice that wills itself to be heard, in many spaces, both private and public, whispered (or shouted) into multiple ears" (560). Indeed, written ten years ago, H.L. Goodall's *Writing the New Ethnography* presents a sensual, rigorous, and embodied method of writing. "Think of the new ethnography," writes Goodall, "as writing that *rhetorically enables intimacy in the study of culture*" (14), a characterization of autoethnographic writing that continues to resonate in his later works (2008). Carolyn Ellis and Art Bochner (2006) advocate a focus on the evocative or emotional elements of autoethnographic writing, a relational ethic that "requires us as researchers to act from our hearts and minds, to acknowledge our interpersonal bonds to others" in autoethnographic work (Ellis 2007, 210).

The conceptualization of autoethnography in *Body, Paper, Stage*, however, is grounded firmly in the disciplinary convergence of performance studies and ethnography; as such, the concept of the "performative-I" will guide the thinking and doing of autoethnography. Victor Turner's concept of performative reflexivity (1986) guides our autoethnographic practice; he states, "Performative reflexivity is a condition in which a sociocultural group, or its most perceptive members acting representatively, turn, bend or reflect back upon themselves, upon the relations, actions, symbols, meanings…social structures and other sociocultural components which make up their public 'selves'" (24). Conceptualized here, the performative-I as based in critical reflections upon self in culture constitutes a significant divergence from the concentration of evocative emotion in the "ethnographic-I" of Ellis's (2003) work. As mentioned in "Bodies of/as Evidence," performance studies has been based in the analysis and embodiment of emotion for centuries. We know that knowledge is evocative, but we do not view the evocation of emotion itself as performatively autoethnographic. Here, a performative-I autoethnography is grounded first and foremost in performativity, meaning it seeks to 1) identify fixed stereotyped categories of gender, race, class and other socially constructed performances, and 2) interrupts these performances with autoethnographies that critique homogenizing categories and the power structures that uphold them, and offer alternatives to dominant and often oppressive ways of being. The personal is inherently political in performance studies.

In performative autoethnography the heart, body, mind, spirit et al. are openly and critically reflective; as such, epistemologies of pain and of hope often emerge. The transdisciplinary desire addressed by alternate methodologies is, I would argue, partially motivated by our want to understand how we know what we know about pain, perhaps to quell it or console it, but at least, to speak it and introduce it into the body of human knowledge. Like bell hooks (1994), "I came to theory desperate, wanting to comprehend—to grasp what was happening in and around me. Most importantly, I wanted the hurt to go away. I saw in theory then a location for healing" (59). It was not until many years after my mother died that I began to write myself out of the stifling pain of her death, embracing the complexities of mother, daughter, identity, class, and other issues (Spry 1997). After years of moving through pain with pen and paper, asking the nurse for these tools the morning after losing our son in childbirth was the only thing I could make my body do. In feeling as if my arms had bounced stiff and clumsily about my ankles that day, the language of bodies came pouring out. Bodies doing and redoing, breaking and remaking meaning is at the core of performative autoethnography.

However, "Pieces" was certainly not written at the bedside of my grieving body. To believe so would be to romanticize the processes of pain and of performative autoethnography. In *Body, Paper, Stage* pain and autoethnography are viewed as a personal/political social praxis, a conflation of the ways in which selves/others interrupt, perpetuate, and are otherwise legislated by dominant cultural systems. The length of the pain I experienced from sexual assault came from my embrasure of the dominant narrative exulting the assault as somehow my fault (1998), or in the case of depression that I must be weak or mentally deficient (2000), or in the case of grief that there was a deadline that I wasn't meeting (2004), or in the case of race that as white I needn't, indeed shouldn't, question privilege (2001b). The more I began to critically reflect upon my own pain, the more I realized the ways it was connected to, and was inherently part of, larger sociocultural pains and confusions. Performative autoethnography is designed to address the kinds of pain that occur at our social/historical/political intersections with one another—the pain caused by our "social ills." Similar to hooks's engagement of theory as a liberatory practice, performative autoethnography invites critical reflection upon pain, creating a space for mutual transformation, hope, and social redress.

Within these sociopolitical intersections, using autoethnography as a method of inquiry inherently sets the subject in the context of her own multiple, heterogeneous, unstable identities where "I" is always and already constructed through a variety of "we." In her work on Red pedagogy, Sandy Grande (2008) articulates a collaborative critical agency in research, "[Red pedagogy] is a space of engagement. It is the liminal and intellectual borderlands where indigenous and nonindigenous scholars encounter one another, working to remember, redefine, and reverse the devastation of the original colonialist 'encounter'" (234). The colonializing historicities of these encounters can be critiqued and transformed through performative autoethnography; they are reassembled from a plural sense of self, a dialectic of copresence where selves and others challenge and recognize their "overlapping cultural identifications" (234) which may be in communion or in conflict with social and power relations. Jazz great Wynton Marsalis writes of deep jazz swing, "It's a matter of understanding what a thing means to you, and being dedicated to playing that even if its meaning casts a cold eye on you yourself" (2005, 59). Marsalis captures the praxis of the performative-I in articulating the necessity for agency as well as accountability. The autoethnographer, who may certainly carry privilege into the research context, must be acutely aware of the power dynamics involved in representation; she must be able to engage in reflexive critique of her own social positioning, must be "dedicated to playing," dedicated to doing reflexivity even, and especially, when her own choices may be the subject of critique.

Bodying Forth

It is a dedication to playing, a fundamental commitment to an embodied communion (pleasant and difficult) with others that I find the sagaciousness of performative autoethnography, a troubled, sensual, contingent embodiment of communitas. Pollock (1998) guides me:

> Entanglement, ravishment, love, writing: what I want to call performance writing does not project a self, even a radically destabilized one, as much as *a relation of being and knowing* that cuts back and forth across multiple 'divisions' among selves, contexts, affiliations…. The self that emerges from these shifting perspectives is, then, *a possibility rather than a fact*, a figure of relation emerging from between lines of difference. (86–87, emphasis mine)

A disposition,

a relation of being and knowing that cuts back,

a possibility

a figure of relation emerging

from difference

from entanglement

from ravishment,

from…

and it is here that I must stop; for to speak of love in relation to research, in an academic

      context,

feels heresy,

not though

in the truth of my "un/learning body" (Madison 2006),

because surely, truly, and ravishingly,

it is love and desire

for communitas, for Burke's consubstantiality, for articulation and interruption of the personally political pains that I inflict on others and that are inflicted upon me within the uneven, unjustified, and inequitable systems privileging some and disempowering others. Heresy or not, it is a disposition of love in autoethnographic research that has given me the courage to move into entanglements with others about race, gender, privilege, and more, resulting in a different kind of knowing, and perhaps in a hope for change.

Ultimately, however varied our voices may be in the articulation of autoethnography, our historical present as researchers is enriched by the constant conversation of what we are doing and why we are doing it. In their introduction to *Ethnographica Moralia: Experiments in Interpretive Anthropology*, Neni Panourgia and George Marcus caution us "not to rest comfortably in our assumptions, in our disciplinary boundaries...but to interrogate their certainty and interrupt their narratives" (3). I rely on the works of James Clifford, Dwight Conquergood, Craig Gingrich-Philbrook, D. Soyini Madison, George Marcus, Della Pollock, Mary Strine, Victor Turner and others who view ethnography as performative, who see, as does Turner (1986), performance as "the explanation and explication of life itself" (21). It is in the *coperformativity of meaning with others* that I find myself as a performative autoethnographic researcher, in the constant negotiation of representation with others in always emergent, contingent, and power-laden contexts. The scholarly desire and pedagogical purpose of this book is reflected in Norman K. Denzin's words:

> Ethnography is not an innocent practice. Our research practices are performative, pedagogical, and political. Through our writing and our talk, we enact the worlds we study. These performances are messy and pedagogical. They instruct our readers about this world and how we see it. The pedagogical is always moral and political; by enacting a way of seeing and being, it challenges, contexts, or endorses the official, hegemonic ways of seeing and representing the other (2006a, 422)

Performative autoethnography radicalizes scholarship through operating under the idea that, as Fabian argues, "In the real world *theory happens*" (2001, 5).

This is why I thank all that is good that I am a performance practitioner. I am thankful to know that we live experience directly, but study it performatively (Spry 2009). I am thankful for the disciplinary wisdom to view lived experience through theories of embodiment and enfleshed methodologies where we learn of something "on the pulses" (Turner in Conquergood 1991, 187) because our bodies are always and already painfully and ecstatically present as we try to understand and articulate "the conditions of our emergence" with others in culture (Butler 2005). It is, as Dwight Conquergood says, a "performance-sensitive way of knowing," (1998, 26) that keeps us dedicated to playing in the messy pedagogical milieu of performative autoethnography.

Questions for Further Consideration:

1. Why is performance not an "added scholarly bonus" in the concept of the textualized body?

2. Why is autoethnography not, as Denzin (2006) says of ethnography, an "innocent practice"?

3. Think of a stereotype about theory or scholarship. How does performative autoethnography challenge that stereotype?

Chapter One

Body

Conceptualizing Performative Autoethnography

Why Do Performative Autoethnography?

In addressing this question, consider the following work first printed in 1997. It contains both the autoethnography (then referred to as autobiography) and the analysis of the autoethnography:

Skins: A Daughter's (Re)construction of Cancer

(A plain straight-backed wooden chair is placed CS. The rest of the stage is bare. Carefully placed over the back of the chair is an opulent full length mink coat. The chair and coat are prelit in a wide dim spot, all else is dark.

The daughter enters slowly from LCS. She is dressed in a classic basic black dress with heels. As she enters, the spot level increases. She very tentatively enters the space delineated by the spot, then walks slowly toward the coat. She circles the coat, touching it gingerly. She picks the coat up to put it on. The coat is heavy in the daughter's hands and she is conflicted about donning the coat.

Finally, she puts it on and is transformed into a carica- tured model on a runway. The daughter/model smiles garishly walking briskly DSC as if modeling and selling the coat; she speaks to the audience.)

Skins

Dead skins

Skins of mothers:

(As mother) "Little...Tami?...Little?..."

Skins of daughters:

(As daughter) "Oh, mom...where are you?..."

(Daughter enacts the action of the narrative as she speaks it.) Do you remember the commercial where the model strides down the runway, takes a big turn at the end of the runway, and as she turns blood comes out of her fur coat

and spatters

the faces

of the audience?

I remember that.

I also remember this:

(In a bright and emotionally distanced tone:) A small hunched woman whose skin is falling from her face and her neck and her body. She is wrapped in these very skins *(indicating the coat)*. On one elbow is a daughter, on the other is a husband.

They help her to the car in the middle of a cold January Michigan winter and whisk her off to the hospital where she dies four days later. After the four days, the daughter wraps herself in these skins. She leaves the hospital, goes to the mother's house, up the stairs into the mother's bedroom, goes into the closet,

(The daughter now begins to embody the described experience as her own:) parts the clothes, and slides down the wall with the clothes around her.

(Crouched DSC) I wrapped these dead skins tight around me and cried for my mother's death, and mourned my life. How would I ever grow new skins now?

And I feel the blood tears on my face as the skins whip around on the final turn of the runway.

(She stands and crosses USC) And I remember this:

(As the mother:) "Now, Little, you need some new clothes. So, you and Mumma will go to lunch and go shopping."

"Oh, Little, that is absolutely darling. Well, you have to have that."

(As saleswoman:) "Oh, Mrs. Spry, your daughter is a perfect size 7."

(As mother, scrutinizing the daughter:) "Gads, she really is."

(As daughter to audience:) Did you see the dignity and power and grace?

(As mother:) "Little, that is absoLUTEly darling."

(As daughter to audience:) My mother died of ovarian cancer when I was 26 years old. And I look just like her—so much so that my grandfather, her father, would not be in the same room with me for two months after she died. My father would come visit us in Southern Illinois and would stand at the door for the first five minutes weeping at the sight of me.

(Crossing US of chair and draping coat over chair) She wrote herself all over this body.

And the cancer did some writing of its own.

I remember this:

(The daughter experiences the narrative action as she speaks it.)

BANG BANG BANG.
I remember waking up in the middle of the night to a
BANG BANG BANG.
It was faint but *very* direct.
My father and I were light sleepers during this time
because my mother had to sleep downstairs in a hospital bed.
She was too weak to climb the stairs.

 BANG BANG BANG.
I went to the top of the stairs and looked down into the darkness. Mom was having trouble sleeping and wanted all the lights off.
I went down the stairs and flipped the hall light on and
BANG BANG BANG...

there was my strong, powerful, beautiful mother
banging on the bed stand with a brush
because she was in too much pain to cry out.

And I remember:

(As mother) "Little, you need some new—" *(As if the sound is going off in the daughter's head.)* BANG BANG BANG

(As mother) "Little that looks absolutely—"

(As daughter, sound building) BANG BANG BANG

(As saleswoman) "Mrs. Spry, your daughter is a perfect size—"

(As daughter, sound building and reaching a crescendo)

BANG BANG BANG.

(Crossing to coat and clutching it, the daughter is afraid, angry, confused.) I clung to these dead skins. But they kept drying up and flaking off. These new ones would appear, but she's not here to initialize them.

(Desperately indicating initials in the coat) Look. BMS. Belle Marie Spry. *(Indicating self)* Who is this woman? Who is this woman whose skins are not notarized by Belle Marie Spry?

(The daughter crosses and places the coat on the chair.) A few weeks after her death, the Black Hole Dreams began.

(She crosses DSC and intimately tells the story to the audience.) The Black Hole Dreams went something like this:

I would come home after a long time at college or a long theatre run. I would come in the back door where Mom would be standing at the top of the stairs. She would say, "Hi, Little!"

Well, in the dreams, I was at the top of the stairs looking down at a black hole. From the hole would come my mother's voice,

"Little...Tami...Little..."

I could never see her,
but I imagined her reaching for me.
And I was too afraid
to go into the black hole
to help her.

Now,
on a bad day,

I cry, "Oh, Ma, come out of there."

(Crossing US to coat and placing hands on coat) But on a good day...
on a good day I say,
"Oh, Ma, come out of there and be with me."

And she does.

(Crossing CS) And she seeps into, through, and all around this body.

And the haunched woman,
and the daughter sinking into the closet,
and Little
and Belle
and Tami
all work to reweave and remake these live skins.

And on a very good day,
you can hear them singing:

"Little...Tami...Little............"

The debut of "Skins: A Daughter's (Re)construction of Cancer" in 1994 at the Speech Communication Association convention in New Orleans marked the beginning of my journey into performing autobiography; it also marked the seventh year of my mother's death from ovarian cancer. I was confused and devastated at her death and tried numerous times to compile a script that would offer myself and others some clarity and insight into

Chapter One ▣ Body: Conceptualizing Performative Autoethnography

this complex experience. However, each time I began to research the experiences of motherless daughters, I would become emotionally paralyzed and artistically bereft. This, of course, only exacerbated the confusion and devastation.

Then, in 1993 a close friend and colleague asked me to contribute to a panel on autobiography. She said, "It's been six years, Tam. Talk about your mom." I did. In my twenty years of performance experience, this was truly the most terrified I had been before a performance. An hour before "curtain" I was in my hotel room sobbing in the arms of two dear friends as I tried in vain to run the show. These women knew my mother Belle, they knew how she had notarized herself upon my body, and knew how I had struggled to be a reliable narrator to her text all of my life. Performing the highly contested relationship between Tami/Belle/Little in the intimacy of our hotel room was more than I could bear. However, I later realized that the public performance of "Skins" would have been impossible without the private cradling by these women as I wept.

Although the performative autobiographical location is a space of intense personal and cultural risk, it is simultaneously a space of profound comfort. It has become for me a site of narrative authority offering me the power to reclaim and rename my voice and body privately in rehearsal, and then publicly in performance. The process enables me to speak about the personally political in public, which has been liberatory and excruciating, but always in some way, enabling. Performative autobiographies are, as Dwight Conquergood (1991) might say, "enabling fictions."

In the process of performing autobiography, the performer concentrates on the body as the site from which the story is generated. She seeks to read what she and others have written on the pulpish hides of her skins. The performative autoethnography process turns the internally *somatic into the externally seman-tic*. I try to coax words out onto the surface of my body. Words write themselves on and in the layers of my skins, introducing me to myself. My reading of those textual pelts becomes the semantic interpretation of my own somatic experience.

In "Skins" I use the body's skin as a unifying and fracturing metaphor for the cultural narratives played out upon bodies. Sidonie Smith articulates the corporeal and conceptual complexity skin suggests when trying to semanticize autobiographic experience:

> Skin is the literal and metaphorical borderland between the materiality of the autobiographical 'I' and the contextual surround of the world. It functions simultaneously as a personal and political, psychological and ideological boundary of meaning....Skin has much to do with autobiographical writing, as the body of the text, the body of the narrator, the body of the narratee, the cultural 'body,' and the body politic all merge in skins and skeins of meaning. (1998, 127–128)

Smith suggests further that the autobiographical subject can find herself outside of her skin, homeless inside her own body. This is certainly an experience I lived after my mother's death. In "Skins" I use my mother's full length mink coat as an iconic symbol of her sociocultural identity that was often illustrated upon my body. I perform:

> (Crossing to mink coat and clutching it, the daughter is afraid, angry, confused.) I clung to these dead skins. But they kept drying up and flaking off. These new ones would appear, but she's not here to initialize them.

> (Desperately indicating initials in the coat) Look. BMS. Belle Marie Spry. (Indicating self) Who is this woman? Who is this woman whose skins are not notarized by Belle Marie Spry? (364)

My life had been largely built around emulating my mother, grafting her skins upon mine. This bodily housing construction *fit the social and ideological specifications of my surround. But a person cannot grow within the hide of another. I was not-me and not-not-me simultaneously (Schechner 1985).*

In performing "Skins" my hide became a corporeal semaphore signaling to myself and others that I was the agent and author of these embodied illustrations. After decades of reading my body according to my mother's authorship, performing autobiography has been a central tool in the reconstitution of my identity. The performing body offers a thick description of an individual's engagement with cultural codes and expectations; it is an ancient scroll upon which is written the stories of one's movement through the world.

This is one example of why I write and perform autoethnography. As mentioned in the analysis of "Skins," through this performance I was able to understand and articulate deeper complexities surrounding my mother's passing. Moreover, following this performance, audience members were anxious to tell me about their own experiences with family members, grief, and healing. Notice, rather than telling me how much they "liked" the performance, the performance generated meaning, ideas, memory in their own lives that they wanted to share. This audience response was deeply transformational for me personally and professionally.

This is an example of why I do performative autoethnography. Why should you?

It is final performance time in my autoethnography class. Students are working on the development of one piece throughout the fifteen week semester. This student, who I will call Amanda, has been working on an autoethnography about the sexual assault she survived in high school. This is her first foray into performance and writing. Her first two instalments of this performative autoethnography were beautifully crafted, and then fully embodied in performance.

In this last development, she had the class get up on stage and stand at the back of the stage facing the wall. She then stood on the floor in front of us where she was three feet below us as we stood on the back of the raised stage looking down. Looking up at us, she began her performance critically reflecting upon where she stands in relation to the assault: looked down upon. She then took autoethnography to task commenting upon what is at stake in excavating pain for critical pedagogies of hope and transformation.

All this while, Amanda had on a backpack. She then told us the last name of her attacker: Lemon. And as she took the backpack off she began to relate an event that happened a few days after the attack. In the middle of her driveway one morning was a brown paper bag. As she opened the bag she found that it was full...of lemons. Students at her school had found out about the attack, and this was their response. As she told us this story, she began reaching into her backpack and handing each of us a lemon. On the lemons were written words. As we read the words, Amanda went into a treatise on the symbology of language, ethics, group think, and the Lucifer Effect (how violent or unethical behaviour becomes normalized within groups). We peeked around at each other's lemons; some said "courage," "insecurity," "power." I was given the last one, "self-reflection." In her last line, still standing three feet below us, she confessed to yet feeling looked down upon, and expressed her desire to someday stand eye-to-eye with others as she thinks about her assault.

Silence.

One of those classroom performances where there is just... silence.

And surely, one of those classroom performances where we allow ourselves to weep.

I swear to you, she was radiant. Radiant during and after the performance. She made this experience HER story, her *analysis*. Her pain. Her hope. Her strength. Her meaning. No longer Lemon's. Hers. And, now, ours.

Self-Other-Context

This is only one of many illustrations of why any of us might invest the time, energy, and *heart* into performative autoethnography. It is important to note that Amanda had never written autoethnography or performed anything before enrolling in this class. It is also important to note that Amanda's work reflects a common level of attainment for students in autoethnography; in other words, this level of writing and performance is attainable through hard work and commitment. The purpose of performative autoethnography is to better understand who we are in relation to others in culture. What does it mean in this world to be Black, wealthy, white, conservative, gay, poor, Muslim, middle-class, elderly? And what do we mean by "this world"? Whose world is it? Who defines it, its norms, values, traditions, and when and where? Or do we experience many worlds/cultures/societies at once, inhabit many social identities at once?

Through performative autoethnography we write ourselves into a deeper critical understanding with others of the ways in which our lives intersect with larger sociocultural pains and privileges. Like critical theorist bell hooks's motivation to theorize, I came to autoethnography from a desire to ease pain and confusion in my life. The more I began to critically self-reflect, the more I realized that my own pain was connected to, and was inherently part of, larger sociocultural pains and confusions of gender, race, class, religion, and more.

The pain of Amanda's experience is met with her own critical analysis of who and where she is in relation to sociocultural attitudes, expectations, and policies of assault. The purpose and potential of performative autoethnography is not to make the pain "go away"; rather, through the process of critically reflecting upon and articulating her account of the experience, she gains an embodied agency, an empowered theorizing, that confronts the terribly embodied feelings of powerlessness accompanying sexual assault. Amanda gains a personally political empowerment through understanding and articulating her connection with others in these large and complex social issues. And, in kind, her story generates connection and meaning in the lives of her audience members. Like so many others, such remains the case for me as I continue to explicate my own experience of sexual assault (Spry 1998).

Connection

Perhaps the most important element in performative autoethnography is *connection*: connection between selves, others, sociocultural context, and the language we use to articulate/represent those connections; it involves connections between personal experience and larger social issues, or, as Judith Butler (2005) contends, accounting for our own emergence in systems of power and privilege. Trinh Mihn-ha agrees with Butler, "Experience, discourse, and self-understanding collide against larger cultural assumptions concerning race, ethnicity, nationality, gender, class, and age" (1991, 157). Performative autoethnography represents the connection between the personal experience and cultural assumptions, between the word and the body, and offers the researcher healing through enacting these connections.

Through my own work over the last ten years, rather than a "self-narrative" as I have argued in the past (2001), I have come to see performative autoethnography as a narrative representing the interrelations and negotiations between selves and others in cultural contexts. The "I" becomes a plural pronoun, a "we" narrative rather than a "me" narrative (Spry 2003). Though communication scholarship has surely established the constative processes of communication, in no other methodology is the coperformativity of socially constructed knowledge more integrally practiced than in performative autoethnography. It is within the power laden entanglements of collaborative knowledge construction that the theory/methodology praxis of performative autoethnography is engaged.

In this chapter we will establish a conceptualization of performative autoethnography that will provide the theoretical underpinning for composing and performing autoethnography. As such, four fundamental and interrelated concepts will be covered that establish the theory/methodology praxis of performative autoethnography: 1) the performative-I disposition, 2) agency and representation, 3) embodiment, and 4) the performance studies classroom. The performative-I disposition is the critical reflective attitude or positionality of the performative autoethnographer. The performative-I disposition is characterized by a heterogeneous subjectivity and a collaborative epistemology. Agency and representation comprise the ethical praxis of performative autoethnography. Agency refers to the act of empowerment in performative autoethnography, while representation refers to the responsibility and accountability of how we represent self and others in writing autoethnography. Embodiment is the theoretical and methodological core of autoethnography and performance, and as such is integral to the performative-I disposition. Knowledge as embodied—for example Amanda's knowledge of sexual assault—is interpreted and articulated through the body rather than from a mind/logic exclusivity. Finally, a brief framing of the performance studies classroom curriculum is addressed as a space of personal/political transformation and change requiring scholarly rigor and personal respect. Remember that although we initially study the body, writing, and performance separately, these processes are epistemologically interdependent in the textualized body.

Performative Autoethnography and the Performative-I Disposition

Performative autoethnography is a *critically reflective narrative* representing the researcher's personal and political intersections/engagements/negotiations with others in culture/history/society. Within this methodology the personal is viewed as inherently political, focusing on the body as coperformative agent in interpreting knowledge. Thinking of the body as coperformative means that we make meaning about ourselves and our lives through our interactions with others. How we interact with family members, friends, and social situations forms the basis of how we make meaning of ourselves and how we think of others and our world. In other words, *we cannot make meaning alone;* thus we argue that our bodies coperform meaning. Performative autoethnography is a narrative articulating how and why and what we think of a particular experience in our lives, how we negotiate the various people and situations.

The construction of this narrative is based upon the researcher's embodiment of a *performative-I disposition in writing, and a performative-I persona in performance* where the researcher engages meaning construction coperformatively with others in culture. It is a negotiation of representation with others in always emergent, contingent, and power-laden contexts; it is a personal accounting of one's social positioning in terms of race, class, gender, etc. The narrative is fluid, always adjusting to the varying conditions of our personal/political lives. In other words, as Amanda's everyday life and interaction with others continues, the meaning she makes about her experience will change, deepen, transform due to the meaning she makes through interaction with others.

Performative autoethnography is a *personal/political social praxis,* and a critically reflexive methodology, meaning it provides a framework to critically reflect upon the ways in which our personal lives intersect, collide, and commune with others in the body politic in ways alternate to hegemonic cultural expectations. It provides a narrative apparatus to pose and engage the questions of our global lives, asking us to embrace one another as fully as we challenge one another.

This narrative apparatus is operationalized through the researcher's movement into a performative-I disposition; it is a location or relation from which the researcher writes a critically reflective narrative about our personal/political intersections. For example, in "Call It Swing: A Jazz Blues Autoethnography," I write about the ways in which my dad both challenged and perpetuated racism in his twenty-five years as a big band jazz drummer:

> My dad's understanding of race resided in the multiple ebb and flow of swing. He was the 'only white boy'when he played with Jimmie Lunceford, and would tell us kids the story of being the only man allowed to enter motels from the front door when

traveling in the South. When I would ask him to recount these experiences, his recollections played somewhere in the 'challenge of time.' [Wynton] Marsalis helps, 'Swing ties in with the heart of the American experience: You make your way; you invent your way. In jazz that means you challenge time, and you determine the degree of difficulty of the rhythms you choose to play. You try to maintain your equilibrium with style, and work within the flow. That's what swing offers' (2005, 48). Though my father spoke of this experience with sadness, and of his band mates with passion and connection, indicating a racial equilibrium on the bandstand, he never recalled protesting when this equilibrium destabilized as he walked through the front door of the motel and his band mates were shuffled to the back. (274)

Notice that the narrative does not *blame* my father for his actions, rather his actions are critiqued through the cultural context within which they took place and the others with whom he interacted. As we will discuss in chapter 3, blame *is not* critical reflection; blame truncates knowledge construction and scholarly inquiry. The performative-I disposition is a methodological location that requires a deep critique of our own motives through a collaborative reflexivity of how and when and where we function in the obvious, obtuse, and invisible systems of power inherent in our everyday lives.

In her 2009 presentation "The Danger of a Single Story," Nigerian author and essayist Chimamanda Adichi recounts how as a girl in Nigeria, her perceptions of the world were formed by British and American literature:

All I had read were books in which characters were foreign, I had become convinced that books, by their very nature, had to have foreigners in them, and had to be about things with which I could not personally identify. Now, things changed when I discovered African books. There weren't many of them available. And they weren't quite as easy to find as the foreign books.

But because of writers like Chinua Achebe and Camara Laye I went through a mental shift in my perception of literature. I realized that people like me, girls with skin the color of chocolate, whose kinky hair could not form ponytails, could also exist in literature. I started to write about things I recognized.

So what the discovery of African writers did for me was this: It saved me from having a single story of what books are. (2)

Adichi's presentation offers an illustration of the ways in which racism and xenophobia are maintained through the danger of having only one view, one opinion, one story of a people, place, or experience. What happens when we base our lives and interactions with others on *one* story?

Performative autoethnography is designed to offer stories alternative to normative taken-for-granted assumptions that clog our understanding about the diversity of experience and systems of power that hold "a single story" in place. Amanda's story of assault, for example, not only contributes to a diversity of cultural notions concerning sexual assault, but also calls into question the denigrating stereotypes of women who speak up and out, women who know intimately the danger of a single story. In short, both Amanda's and Chimamanda's stories becomes pedagogical and transformative for listeners, opening a space for personal healing, public dialogue, and policy changes.

> Think of a time when you felt limited by a single story. How did this story affect your thoughts about yourself, about others, about your community?

A performative-I disposition incorporates performativity in identifying dominant normalized performances of race, gender, class (Butler 1997, Madison and Hamera 2006), and then interrupts and intervenes on these oppressive norms through creating alternative and transgressive autoethnographic performativities. As mentioned earlier, performativity involves 1) identifying fixed stereotyped categories of gender, race, class and other socially constructed performances, and 2) interrupting these performances with autoethnographies that critique these categories and the power structures that uphold them. "Performativity," write Madison and Hamera, "is the interconnected triad of identity, experience, and social relations.... Performativities are the many markings substantiating that all of us are subjects in a world of power relations" (xix). Performative autoethnography attempts to critically interrupt dominant narratives of our "many markings" by offering a performance that breaks normative patternized behaviours and remakes stories that transgress dominant power relations. For example, in "Call It Swing," I try to offer various ways of accounting for my father's behaviour based on analyzing who he may have been within that cultural and historical context.

The performative-I disposition invites us toward an examination of how we *coperformatively function* within a particular sociocultural/political/historical context to (re)make meaning that illustrates the complex dialogical negotiations between selves and others in cultural contexts. The autoethnographer seeks to articulate the collisions and collaborations with others as we traverse cultural norms and expectations together, provoking critical reflection upon differences in power and privilege for personal and political transformation.

Agency and Representation

The stories that emerge in each case rise up against the norms that deny their integrity, that prefer silence, conformity, and invisibility. In the corporealities of performance, they break through normative reiteration into the time-space of terrifying exhilarating possibility.

Della Pollock, *Telling Bodies Performing Birth*, 27–28

Engaging a performative-I disposition, the student is made aware that this is *her* story; though our process of critical reflection is coperformative, no one gets to *tell* this story but her. No one gets to construct this narrative but her, not the media, not the social worker, not the councillor, not her friends, boyfriend, or her mother or father. Though these peoples and cultural mechanisms are involved in the coperformative meaning Amanda makes, autoethnography gives her permission, gives her the space, the time, the *right* to critically reflect and carefully craft the story of her experience, a story that indeed might "rise up against the norms that deny their integrity." In other words, in the process of writing her story through the method of performative autoethnography, Amanda has *agency* in the constructing/writing/telling of her story. In "Skins," I had to figure out who I was without my mother's presence in the world, who I am without having her to identify with; I had to tell my own story of identity.

Agency refers to the capacity of the agent (in this case an individual) to tell her story of an event, also keeping in mind that the construction of the story is generated from the individual's sociocultural situatedness, or how she constructs and is constructed by social systems such as race, class, gender, religion, etc. So, Amanda may become personally and politically empowered by telling *her* story of the assault, in this case, constructing the story to illustrate how unequal power dynamics of gender function to provide and perpetuate a culture of sexual assault. In *Storytelling in Daily Life: Performing Narrative*, authors Kristin Langellier and Eric Peterson cite the example of Marie who "uses her story to 'talk back' to the institution of the Roman Catholic church....It is unlikely that such institutions will ever actually 'hear' this story. Instead, they function as a virtual addressee for Marie's story" (12), providing Marie empowerment through critical reflection, and providing her audience with an alternate story of being Catholic. Like Marie, Amanda constructs her individual experience to critique larger social systems of power, and in doing so, gains definitional agency through representing herself as taking power, taking representational

control over how her assault is perceived, thus interrupting dominant narratives of sexual assault "that prefer silence, conformity,
and invisibility" (Pollock 1999, 128).

A dialectical agency characterizes the performative-I disposition. Although Amanda is the author of her story, the story is a
collection of representational fragments of knowledge assembled
with others from a plural sense of self, a dialectic of copresence
with others concerning how bodies are read in various contexts of
culture and power. In her essay "Performing Writing," Della Pollock describes a performative self that "is not merely multiple," it
moves itself "forward...and between selves/structures" (1998, 87).
A performative-I disposition is less concerned with individual identity and more concerned with constructing a representation of the
conflictual effects of coperforming meaning with others.

In speaking of Conquergood's concept of dialogical performance, Madison writes, "Dialogue is framed as performance to
emphasize the living communion of a felt-sensing, embodied interplay and engagement between human beings" (2005, 9), a kind
of engagement that speaks into difficulties or conflictual effects
of social conflict. How are our perceptions of others or of power
affected by a dialogical engagement with others, usurping the danger of a single story? Vershawn Ashanti Young illustrates dialectic
agency in *Your Average Nigga: Performing Race, Literacy, and Masculinity* where he seeks to "illustrate the intersection between what
I call the burden of racial performance and the problems that I and
other blacks face in the ghetto and in school, particularly in college" (2007, 12). This kind of performative-I identification does
not romanticize collaboration or assume that autoethnography is a
manifestation of agreement or consensus or solution or emotional
connection between selves and others. Rather than empowerment
through asking "Why can't we all just get along?," dialectic agency
is gained through critically reflecting upon the question and producing a variety of possibilities of how we might move forward.

Within critical agency is the ethical awareness of representing one's own reflection upon the complex intersections and negotiations between selves and others in power-laden contexts.

Grounded in the "crisis of representation," issues of *representation* provide a check and balance in the ethics of agency in performative autoethnography. Surely, performative autoethnography provides the opportunity for personal empowerment; *however,* the performative-I disposition requires that in representing her story, the agent is responsible for and answerable to her representation of others in the autoethnographic context. The way in which we represent people, places, cultures through writing illustrates the values, beliefs, biases, and perspectives held by the writer in this case, the auto-ethnographer. The performative-I disposition assumes the inherency of accountability in

> What are the social conditions of your emergence? How has race, financial status, gender, or other social conditions affected your view of yourself and others? How has it affected your interactions? How might you represent these interactions?

autoethnography. "There is no 'I'," writes Butler, "that can stand apart from the social conditions of its emergence" (2005, 7). I do not stand apart from the privileges of my whiteness, physical ability, or financial status. These social conditions always inhabit the form and content of any autoethnography I might produce.

Thus, as the *critically self-reflective* agent of her experience, Amanda must also understand herself as answerable for how she represents self, others, and culture in her autoethnographic writing. This embeddedness of critical reflection upon one's social conditions is what makes performative autoethnography *performative*; it is the foundation of a performative-I disposition. As mentioned earlier, performative autoethnography is designed to critique, to call into question normative patterns of behavior that perpetuate oppressive power structures and dominant cultural narratives. Since the autoethnographer creates a version of reality through writing (representation), she is, then, responsible for the reality she creates. She must be answerable to it and accountable for it. Judith Butler refers to this as "giving an account of oneself." She writes:

> When the 'I' seeks to give an account of itself, it can start with itself, but will find that this self is already implicated in a social temporality that exceeds its own capacities for narration: indeed when the 'I' seeks to give an account of itself, an account that must include the conditions of its own emergence, it must, as a matter of necessity, become a social theorist. (8–9)

We construct categories of race, gender, religion, etc. through the language we use. That language reflects cultural values and hierarchies that perpetuate or deconstruct, that install or interrupt systems of power. So, though performative autoethnography may be empowering, Amanda is also responsible for giving "an account of herself," a self that is—as we all are in various ways—already implicated in larger systems of power, and must, therefore, produce a text that includes the conditions of her emergence in these social systems. The performative autoethnographer is, in Butler's sense, a social theorist, one who dialectically engages personal experience to critically theorize about larger social issues. It is in Amanda's knowledge of the power of aesthetic production (of writing) as representation that she not only becomes the empowered agent of self representation, but also understands herself as responsible for the power in representations of otherness. In other words, representation has risks.

The ethical guidelines and possible ethical pitfalls involved in representing self and other are directly addressed in Conquergood's foundational article, "Performing as a Moral Act: Ethical Dimensions of the Ethnography of Performance" (1985). He conceptualizes ethnography and performance as dialogical, where performer and text challenge and embrace one another, where agency and representation must work collaboratively for an ethical performance. This process is located in the textualizing body where critical reflection, composition, and performance work in concert and in dissonance with one another. A comprehensive method of composing an ethical autoethnography is explicated in chapter 3: Composing Performative Autoethnography.

Agency and representation are a dialectic check and balance for the ethics of autoethnography. While at once empowered by the agency of constructing the story, the performative autoethnographer is also aware that the way she represents that story through language and performance is inherently a politically contested and personally accountable process. "Representation" writes Madison, "happens at different points along power's spectrum—we are all 'vehicles and targets' of power's contagion and omnipresence" (2009, 193). The performative-I disposition encourages the researcher to locate self in relation to others in the both/and of "power's contagion" seeking to understand how we—as both vehicles and targets—can effectively negotiate and transform power's contagion, and to continually inoculate ourselves against the danger of a single story.

Embodiment

I could tell a white band from a black band. I could just tell, it wouldn't go into my body.

Miles Davis, "The Miles Davis Story," a documentary

Davis's words illustrate the corporeal embeddedness of knowledge. They reveal the inherency, the seamlessness, the materiality of the personal and political, in a manner where we cannot tell where one ends and the other begins. His words speak a theory of *embodiment*, a theorizing of the embodied knowledge of, among other things, race. He could just "tell," his body telling, his telling body, that a particular composition wouldn't "go into my [his] body," not because he didn't *know* or understand the sound, but perhaps because he knew it too well, was *required* to know it, knew it as a racially compulsory verse in the soundscapes of power, where the oppressed are required to know more about the oppressor for their own survival. It is in the agency of *telling*, of the telling body, in the critical assignment of language to experience, that performative autoethnography is constructed (Spry 2010). This is the basic foundation of autoethnography, the pulse of this methodology of the heart (Pelias 2005), the peril of this anthropology that will break your heart (Behar 1997).

In performative autoethnography the researcher concentrates on the body as the site from which the story is generated by turning the internally *somatic* into the externally *semantic* (Spry 2003). Embodied knowledge is the somatic (the body's interaction with culture) represented through the semantic (language), a linguistic articulation, a telling, of what does and does not go into the body, and why. But whose body? Whose words? Where/who does the telling come from? What is the sociocultural and temporal location and implication of the researcher, of the autoethnographer? What is the relationship between autoethnographer and others when considering and employing embodied theory and methodologies (embodied praxis)? The politics of/in the body are central in performative autoethnography; Madison writes:

> In performance studies we do a lot of talking about the body. For performance ethnographers, this means we must embrace the body not only as the feeling/sensing home of our being— the harbor of our breath—but the vulnerability of how our body must move through the space and time of another—transporting our very being and breath—for the purpose of knowledge, for the purpose of realization and discovery. (2009,191)

Embodied knowledge is the research home, the methodological toolbox, the "breath" of the performative autoethnographer. It allows the researcher to reflect upon the myriad ways in which, for example, Davis's statement is packed with the politics of race, the politics of his body as the home of his being. It is, among other things, his social/cultural/temporal embodiment as a distinguished musician, as an African-American man, and as a person raised in financial privilege that embodies the ways in which he, and we as readers, make meaning of his words.

Embodied knowledge is knowledge that is gained by paying close somatic attention to how and what our body feels when inter-acting with others in contexts. The knowledge is articulated through a performative-I disposition where the researcher critically reflects upon what and where the body *knows*. Surely my own scholarship, and this book itself, is generated through a performative-I disposi-tion. In fact, in the methodological fashion of autoethnography, the emergence of a performative-I concept was the result of a deep and all-consuming loss and the necessity to save my life after death.

Engaging the body as a source of knowledge after a traumatic loss brought about the concept of a performative-I copresence (Spry 2006). All understandings of research and life broke apart for me into pieces large and small, sharp edged, inchoate, and seemingly irretrievable after the loss of our son in childbirth in 2002. Writing was the only thing I could make myself do. My arms literally ached from the absence. I felt dismembered mentally and physically, phan-tom limbs holding a baby, "shards of language" falling about me. My subject position went from a destabilized "me" to a chaotic but oddly comforting "we." And because, as bell hooks suggests, theory heals, Sidonie Smith's words acted as balm:

> And so the cultural injunction to be a deep, unified, coherent, autonomous "self" produces necessary failure, for the auto-biographical subject is amnesiac, incoherent, heterogeneous, interactive. In that very failure lies the fascination of autobio-graphical storytelling as performativity. (1998, 108)

"Paper and Skin: Bodies of Loss and Life" is the performative autoethnographic result. It is a "necessary failure" of a coherent uni-fied self. In Smith's concept of autobiographical performativity, the autobiographical subject is not an intact coherent self waiting within the body to be recorded through language; rather, she is a conflation of effects, a "constellation of resources" created through a performa-tive process of critical narration that resists notions of individual coherency; the performative-I disposition is a coupling of this sense of subjective incoherency with critical ethnographic reflexivity.

Rupture and Fragmentation

After much frustration with dominant cultural narratives of grief as well as my own writing process at the time, I finally gave in to the rupture of a coherent "I." In their call for a "deconstructive auto-ethnography," Jackson and Mazzei (2008) argue for an "I" that confronts "experience as questionable, as problematic, and as incomplete—rather than as a foundation for truth" (304). Rather than seeking endings or answers, it was in the comfort of incoherency and incompleteness that I began to find relief. The performative-I disposition is about living in the body of the question rather than answering it.

Through engaging knowledge as embodied, I began to experience rupture and fragmentation as a form and function of performative ethnographic representation. In her deeply moving book *Telling Bodies Performing Birth,* Della Pollock speaks with women whose stories of birth suggest such rupture. Their stories "bend to the breaking point the comic-hero norm of birth storytelling, making story answer to performance, performance to difference, and difference to its origins in absence, in silence, in the blank expanse of not knowing and unknowing that remains impenetrably unknown" (1999, 27–28). As I let myself fall apart, I let myself see the pieces. I let myself fall into the presence of absence, into "the blank expanse of not knowing." My own experience of the multiplicity and partiality of knowledge became deeply embodied; I understood this as an autoethnographic stance, as a construction of self that seemed to navigate, to negotiate the interrelations between self/other/bodies/language/culture/history in ways that were markedly different from any previous "I" positionality in my research. Butler writes:

> I speak as an 'I,' but do not make the mistake of thinking that I know precisely all that I am doing when I speak in that way. I find that my very formation implicates the other in me, that my own foreignness to myself is, paradoxically, the source of my ethical connection with others. (2005, 84)

Relating to our discussion of representation, Butler suggests a decentering of epistemological authority in the "I" of autoethnographic writing. This decentering of authority made great sense walking in the fragments and rubble of loss personally in our family and nationally in 9/11. Any sense of knowledge located firmly within the boundaries of my own body fell away, and I began to feel within the concept of performativity and copresence, an engagement with others in culture that was no longer centered in "I." As Conquergood (1991) contends, performance is about the struggle to push through what seems fixed, static, or hopeless. My emptied body needed to speak of absence, of the incoherence of here/now/

> Think of an experience where your body holds the depth of knowledge of that experience.

who, to embody, as Ruth Bowman (2005) said, "inconsistency as a form of knowledge," "to expose," write Jackson and Mazzei (2008), "the indecidability of meaning, of self, of narrative—without requiring self-identification or mastery" (305). Moving from the notion of a "deep autonomous selfhood" into the deconstructive motile vision of empty arms falling began and structured the piece-meal form of "Paper and Skins: Bodies of Loss and Life."

In-and-Between Bodies

From this embodied negotiation with others in loss emerged a performative-I disposition. Grief and autoethnography began to make a more deeply embodied and more problemitized "felt-sense" (Bacon 2008). Seeking embodied knowledge through a performative-I disposition with others takes us out of a *singular* body in the same way as autoethnography takes us out of a single story. Engaging knowledge as collaborative pushes and pulls us into the liminal inbetweeness of meaning making with others, "The gaze [of the researcher] is always shifting inward, outward, and throughout the spaces-in-between" (233), writes Sandy Grande (2008), a place and time defined by the multiple and surely conflictual readings of our cultural situatedness and the meanings we make coperformatively/together. A performative-I embodied disposition shifts us into the void between our material bodies where we meet each other in dialogue, in argument, in communion, in anger, in the *mysterium tremendum* that performance studies scholar Leland Roloff (1973) describes where cultural presence is what our bodies in contexts are making together. Here we are performatively *doing* the personal politics of culture through embodiment.

In moving out of self and into a performative troubled communion with others, we have the opportunity to look beneath the skin of our own privilege, oppression, pain, and hubris and into the possibility of a "utopian performative," articulated by performance scholar Jill Dolan, "a different future, one full of hope and reanimated by a new, more radical humanism" (2005, 5). Madison's work on a "dangerous ethnography" develops communal embodiment with others as a path toward a "performative utopia"; she writes, "We are not only participant-observers with Others, but flesh-to-flesh coperformative witnesses in the risky business of a contagious desire, passion, and urgency that affects us all, propelling back and forth between us/among us through our feeling/sensing vulnerable bodies" (2009, 195). It is, I would guess, a contagious desire for hope that moves us through grief, 9/11, Katrina, war, and the everyday stumbles and embrasures of living in, learning in, and transforming the inequality of our everyday lives.

> Briefly describe one or two difficult experiences in your life that might be transformed into reasons for hope.

An embodied disposition of performative-I autoethnography involves personal/political risk by situating us in the space between self/other/bodies/culture/language where we do not have the "safety" of "I," where we are vulnerable to contestation with others about what is what, about the critical readings and representations of bodies. For example, in seeking to represent how my friend and colleague, she Kenyon and Black, and I American and white, negotiate our movement through the un/conscious racism of the Academy, it is living in the inbetweeness of self/other/bodies/culture/language that I see my "outrage" at the racism visited upon her daily as privilege, and her silence as strategy (Spry 2008). Whether I am reflexive or not, I do not shed my white skin in the "auto" of ethnography like a pelt of privilege that I can take on and off. As my colleague and I have often confronted, her brown skin and my white skin do not change color simply because we are critically reflective, but in an embodied performative-I disposition, where we move out of a singular self and into the communicative space between us, the dominant narratives defining those colors can be interrupted and retold, metamorphosizing language's propensity toward imperializing.

I see the power implications of privilege by critiquing my own performance of privilege in relation to and with my friend. Rather than expecting her, as a person of color, to "teach" me, a white person, about racism, through performative autoethnography I try to take the responsibility to account for the social conditions of my own emergence within a system of white privilege, within academia, and within our friendship. Trinh Minh-ha writes, *"We will have to face these issues of modern subjectivity,...such as* responsibility *within a context of uneasy conscience where one realizes one is often the oppressor of someone else"* (1991, 114, emphasis in text). In coming out of a singular self, we have the opportunity to confront our own hubris, privilege, oppression, and pain as they are always and already connected to others. It is, as Madison states, "the wonderful paradox in the ethnographic moment...that communion with the Other brings the self more fully into being and, in doing so, opens you to know the Other more fully" (2005, 9). I know and can transform oppression more fully in looking at the performance of my own body as in communion and/or conflict with others.

Surely and without question, within a performative-I disposition, I am critically and unromantically aware that no matter how liminally out of my body I may move, it is a racially and financially privileged body that I live in. And surely, it has been from stumbling, bumbling, and wounding others unconsciously and otherwise within my own racial privilege that I continually check myself. In an earlier work, "From Goldilocks to Dreadlocks," I try, in varying degrees of success, to critique these stumbles and wounds while harkening to Trinh's warning: "It is always mindboggling to recognize how readily opposed liberal Westerners are to any discrimination in the public treatment of people of color while remaining blind to it in more individualized relationships or when dealing with difference on a one-to-one basis" (1991, 158). Through the performative-I disposition, the researcher might articulate the complexity of cultural interaction, how the researcher's uses of dominant discourse affect these interactions, how we are all, as Madison suggests, "'vehicles and targets' of power's contagion and omnipresence" (2009, 193). The complexities of cultural interaction constitute the reasons and need for the critical imagination (Denzin 2006) necessary to move out of a singular body and into the rapture and entanglements of what Conquergood (1991) calls a "performance sensitive" way of knowing to articulate and transform dominant narratives that sediment systems of power.

We do not enter these spaces lightly or stumble into this process without strategy, without method, without a practice. The performative-I disposition is wholly dependent upon performative embodiment where the textualizing body is the actor, agent, and text at once, where our views of the world are tested, refuted, and articulated through the negotiation of corporeal bodies in space and time. It is a "bodying forth" (Papagaroufali 2008) into critical social theorizing where the resulting text causes interruption, refutation, and intervention upon dominant narratives.

The performative-I disposition braids performativity, agency and representation, and embodiment into an ethic of negotiation with others' bodies, contexts, temporalities. While autoethnography is performative/pedagogical/embodied/accountable, it is also in the service of simultaneously deconstructing what it might be putting together, which is, for me, the continual process of critical reflection (Spry 2009). It is, definitely, a nervous condition, as Pollock (1998) decries, but, paradoxically, this performative-I disposition has offered me fragmentation as pedagogy, brought me presence in the absence of life, and serves as a constant check of my own privileged hubris.

The Performance Studies Classroom and Beyond

In a January 2010 issue of the New York Times, Garth Saloner, the dean of the Graduate School of Business at Stanford University made a sweeping curriculum change. He said, "If I'm going to really launch you on a career or path where you can make a big impact in the world, you have to be able to think critically and analytically about the big problems in the world" (1). Titled "Multicultural Critical Theory; At Business School?" the article discusses changes in the core curriculum of top business schools to include "learning how to think critically... how to imaginatively frame questions and consider multiple perspectives." Saloner's comments reflect the common trend in business schools and professional communities of engaging the complexity of diversity through creativity and critical thinking—two of the most foundational concepts in performance studies curriculum. Performance ethnographer Dwight Conquergood concurs:

> This epistemological connection between creativity, critique, and civic engagement is mutually replenishing, and pedagogically powerful. Very bright, talented students are attracted to programs that combine intellectual rigor with artistic excellence that is critically engaged, where they do not have to banish their artistic spirit in order to become a critical thinker, or repress their intellectual self or political passion to explore their artistic side. (2004, 319–320)

The performance studies curriculum reaches beyond the classroom, providing practical and intellectual needs of our public and civic lives and careers. I am continually heartened to know that students in performance studies classrooms are being equipped to engage and transform global challenges—the financial collapse of this decade for example—through methods that see these challenges as personally political rather than as a distanced financial spreadsheet. Surely, the financial collapse could be viewed as resulting from the danger of a single story. In researching this event, the performative autoethnographer might analyze the personally political connections of self/other/context in relation to financial systems of power and privilege by creating another story, an alternative story that may reveal subaltern power structures that seek to control people's access to financial security. Imagine a performative autoethnography from a member of a family caught in the web of a big bank's proctoring of bad loans for their own gain. Personal experience braided with critical reflection and research on the financial crisis would offer a moving complex analysis of the costs of unbridled and unethical power structures.

In fact, many leaders in non-profit organizations and business have come to rely upon autoethnography as a deeply transformational means of training speakers and advocates. For example, communication consultants John Capecci and Timothy Cage train advocates and spokespeople to tell their stories having made the "important decision to share personal experiences publicly for the benefit of others or on behalf of a cause or policy, for anyone who hopes that one person's story can help move audiences to action." In their forthcoming book *Living Proof: Telling Your Story to Make a Difference,* Capecci and Cage explain the value of telling one's story for the purpose of advocacy and social change:

> Every day, at rallies and fundraisers, in radio and television studios, in community centers, on the phone with local print journalists, and in front of web cameras, millions of individuals like you are coming forward to tell their stories. They speak to raise awareness, change minds, influence public policy, educate, mobilize, give voice to under- or misrepresented

people, promote a beneficial product or service, and raise money. They speak for causes both local and global—from creating safer streets to reducing the risk of heart disease in women, from improving neighborhood recycling initiatives to ending homelessness. They tell their stories with humor, anger, hope, candor, and passion. They are going public with their personal and sometimes intimate experiences... because they believe that by doing so, they can help others and make a positive change in the world. (xxi)

This is just one of the many ways that performative autoethnography operates outside of the classroom and into public and professional spheres. Our stories allow us to understand one another and move us to see one another as allies for a better world no matter where we might stand ideologically.

The performance studies classroom is a space of transformation and change built upon the engagement of creativity, critique, and culture. As we have discussed thus far, the performative-I disposition is culturally coperformative, meaning that knowledge is forged with others in recognizing and critiquing our various culturally constructed privileges and marginalizations; it is critically reflective, requiring analysis of our own beliefs, values, and sociocultural expectations; and it is creative, requiring us to move out of our personal/cultural comfort zone to produce knowledge through aesthetic means. The performance studies classroom is, as Nathan Stucky notes, a space of "personal and social discovery" as well as theoretic and artistic practice (2006, 262). Performance studies creates a space, a context, where students feel the agency to explore and critique their own "social emergence" as it communes and collides with others in the context of larger social issues.

Transformation and change on a personal and social level requires a *radical pedagogy* where the body is perceived as the central component in knowledge creation rather than a disembodied "mind" into which an educator pours knowledge (Freire 1970, McLaren 2004, Pineau 2002). In the performance studies classroom, "teaching and learning are fundamentally somatic processes" (Pineau 2002, 49) creating space for a "performance of possibilities" (Madison 2009) where, through performance, students realize a multitude of possibilities in human behavior and cultural understanding. Conceptualizing performance as a process of possibilities prevents the "danger of a single story" through students engaging, embodying, and enacting ways of being that flesh out many stories of human being.

As in any form of change, however, there is much at stake for the student in "radicalizing" the classroom through engaging the personal as political. This is why, as we consider the embodiment of the performative-I disposition in the following chapters, we do not take the responsibility of performance pedagogy lightly.

Karen's analysis of a family member's suicide.

Carl's experience of surviving cancer.

William's critical reflection on racial differences in homophobia.

Anthropologist Victor Turner (1986) argues that performance is the explanation and explication of life itself. So what is at stake for these students while explicating their lives in the performance classroom? What is at stake for students when engaging the vulnerable, transformative, and dangerous terrain of critical performative autoethnographic performance, particularly and especially when they are not prepared with a theory/methodology praxis grounded in the discipline of performance studies? What are the rights of students in this pedagogical performance process, and how are these pedagogical rights violated by a lack of substantive preparation in a performance praxis? Though the names are changed, the examples above come directly from my own autoethnographic performance classroom. Clearly, as Conquergood (1985) argues, performance is a moral act, and as Denzin (2002) argues, autoethnography is a moral discourse, meaning that we engage the array of deeply held values and beliefs developed through our families and communities, and through governmental, educational, and other societal structures. In performative autoethnography, students identify and analyze the moral construction and sociocultural expectations that structure their identities with others. What is at stake for an African-American student in a majority white classroom, for the female student reflecting on poverty, for the GLBT student who may be coming out in the critical reflections of homophobia? Knowledge is not innocent or apolitical. Much is potentially at stake in a performative that "does not simply observe but bears the responsibility of witnessing, and it does not simply participate but embodies performance with a deeply felt sensing empathy" (Madison 2009, 195).

It is thus an ethical imperative for students to be provided the theoretical and methodological foundation in the study of performance when asked to engage the vulnerable, transformational, and moral terrain of critical autoethnographic performance. "The critical imagination," writes Denzin, "is radically democratic, pedagogical, and interventionist" (2006, 331); living within an unequal system of power requires a critical imagination for the purposes of radicalizing hope and materializing peace. The performance studies classroom is a space of ethical care manifested through rigorous study and respect; it is a space of mutual care for one another and for the potential of performance to open up the world.

In this chapter we have engaged the question of why one might do performative autoethnography. We established a performative-I disposition as the perspective that one might take in critically reflecting upon the personal/political implications of experiences with others in our everyday lives. And most importantly, we establish performative autoethnography as a process of generating meaning in articulating how we are connected with others in sociocultural contexts of pain and joy. It is, as Wynton Marsalis (2005) says, a dedication to playing, even, and especially when, we must be the subjects of our own sociocultural accounting.

Questions for Further Consideration

1. How would you answer the question that opens this chapter: "Why do performative autoethnography?"

2. In conceptualizing the performative-I disposition, describe the difference between a "me" narrative and a "we" narrative. Provide an example of the difference.

3. How does the check and balance of agency and representation ensure ethical representation of self and others?

4. What elements of the performance studies classroom might prepare students for constructive engagement in a multicultural community, either personally, professionally, or both? Explain.

Chapter Two

Paper
Writing the Body

I only write or make art about myself when I am completely sure that the biographical paradigm intersects with larger social and cultural issues.

Guillermo Gomez-Pena
Dangerous Border Crossers: The Artist Talks Back, 7

Every woman's confessional narrative has more meaningful power of voice when it is well crafted.

bell hooks
Remembered Rapture: The Writer at Work, 68

☞ A personal story told to a friend over coffee.

☞ A written passage describing the emotions accompanying the loss of someone close.

☞ A critique of systemic racism and cultural forms of oppression.

These are all important stages in the construction of performative autoethnography. They are elements in the *content* of performative autoethnography. But they are not in themselves performative autoethnography.

As we move into a discussion of writing, consider the following autoethnography and its accompanying analysis first printed in 2000.

Tattoo Stories: A Postscript to "'Skins"

(Performer stands DSC. She is wearing a sleeveless funky-chic flowing dress that highlights the tattoo on her upper-left arm. She wears a shawl animated with suns, moons, and stars. She is bare-footed. A straight backed chair with no arms is placed center stage. The stage is otherwise bare.)

But

on a good day...

on a good day I say,

"Oh, Mom, come out of there and be with me."

And she does.

And she seeps into, through, and all around this body.

(The performer enacts the following images through movement.)

And the haunched woman,

and the daughter sinking into the closet,

and Little

and Belle

and Tami

all work to reweave and remake these new skins.

And on a *very good* day,

you can hear them singing:

"Little... Tami... Little............. "

So ended a performative autobiography that I first performed
in 1994 at the Speech Communication Association in New
Orleans called "Skins: A Daughter's (Re)Construction of Cancer." I wore heels, hose, and a tailored black dress imported
from Italy. It was the dress that I wore to my mom's funeral.

This autobiographical performance is called "Tattoo Stories",

and is just one continuation

of "Skins."

*(Performer crosses UL and re-enters the stage powerfully and
playfully singing a funky rhythm. Throughout this play with
the audience, she somewhat coyly flashes her tattoo hidden by
her shawl. Finally with great flourish, she reveals the tattoo
on her upper left arm and makes a muscle for the audience.
She then crosses to the chair and lays her shawl across it.)*

My mother died 10 years ago last month.

She cut a beautiful,

dignified,

and dominating

figure.

She wore a full length mink coat;

it was iconic of who she was.

It symbolized her struggle from poverty

into a life of comfort,

a journey from a family of chaos

into our family's regimented control.

And Mom

was the overseer,

the sergeant,

and the sage.

(Performer engages movement reflecting the following images as she speaks.)

It has taken me these ten years to shed that coat, [she begins taking it off slowly, tentatively, with difficulty]

to peel off those skins, [the coat becomes harder to take off, she peels it off her arms]

and to find out who else

she and I are [the coat is off; she is tentative but anticipatory]

underneath.

One year ago January,

another layer of skin fell away

and underneath was this [gesture to tattoo]

It just

emerged one day.

The artist

who happened to be there

when it happened

said that she could

feel it writing itself

as if it were surfacing

from a space

in my body

dark

and

deep.

The outer design is the Celtic symbol for the Tree of Life. In Pagan spiritualities, the tree is a sacred symbol of life, circularity, fertility, and creativity. Inside the body of the tree are two women dancing—something like this. [she lifts her right arm over her head and lifts her left leg; she then leans back gracefully]

But as the tattoo continued to grow out of me,

writing itself from that dark and deep space,

I became more and more unclear

as to whether the women were dancing, [she enacts the above movement]

or kicking, [from the dance position she uses her left leg to angrily kick]

or falling. [the kick causes her to fall off balance; she catches herself before falling to the floor]

Now, I rather like this ambiguity

because I am never quite sure if *I*

am dancing,

or kicking,

or falling.

But up until a couple of years ago,

I was *very* sure.

In my family growing up,

one must always at least *appear*

as if

she were dancing.

*(During the next passages the performer confidently and
proficiently enacts complicated formal ballet movements and
positions.)*

One must always be

in control—

always disciplined.

One could kick if she were angry;

but it was always understood

that this was just a different kind

of control.

In my family,

if you were not in control,

you risked people seeing your weaknesses and vulnerabilities.

And that that was *never, ever*

appropriate.

So I worked very hard

to make everyone   believe

that I was always dancing,

       always   *in*   *control.*

(The dancing stops.)

Two and a half years ago,

after 34 years of disciplined dancing

and angry kicking...

I finally fell.

Two and a half years ago
I had a mental breakdown,
a breakthrough,
a deconstruction
and reclamation
of the most intimate kind.
It was a most terrifying,
    ecstatic,
        and euphoric

            dance of selves.

The process of falling was slow, [she begins walking in a large circle center stage; she seems worried and unable to stop her movement]

but not gentle.

It was punc [her torso spasms and contracts forward and backward] tuated with

fits [again]   and   starts, [again]

far from the disciplined dance that I was used to.

(Performer shifts to a flashback of the breakdown. She is walking/stumbling in a circle on stage, talking on the phone.) Um, um... Deb... ah, um, I, um... Deb?

(Performer shifts back to present time.)

During those last days, I saw many faces.

Some were the faces of my mom:

(Performer sits and talks with a fictional other using off stage focus. She tells the story as if it is humorous, as if it is "no big deal.")

Um, Marla, did I ever tell you about this one thing my mom used to tell me? When I was little, like three, and four, and five, up until I was a teenager, my mom used to tell me that I wasn't really hers, that I wasn't really her child and that my real father was the garbage man and that he might come to get me some day. And she would go on to say that she found me one day in the garbage can... and that she took me in. And it was like this family joke, that she wasn't really my real mom, and that I was the garbage man's kid and that he could show up any day. It was supposed to be this funny joke. And when I was very young—before I had learned that it was funny—my mom would go on about it until I started to cry. And then she would laugh and say, "Oh, no. Not really, not really." But even though it was supposed to be this family joke... um... she was usually the only one there...

Isn't that funny?

(Back to present audience.) And my friend Marla said, "Oh, Tami."

And my friend Laila said, "Oh, honey."

And I was surprised by their somber reactions.

Well, I told my therapist, Carole, this story because she seemed really interested in my mom. Even though I kept telling her that my mom was this wonderful person, she kept asking me about my mom. And since she had diagnosed me as severely clinically depressed I thought I should give her something, so...

I told her.

And

as I told her...

I started to sob.

I started to sob

those deep gut-twisting sobs.

And I couldn't stop.
And she put her hand on my knee
as I fell
and fell
and fell.

(Flashback to breakdown. Again on phone.)

Um, um, um, Carole? Um... I... I... um, I... I don't know.
Carole? Um...

(Back to present.)

And on the way down,

I saw the face of my grandmother.

(As mother talking to performer. Use on stage focus.)

Little, Little, come on. Come on, wake up.

(Performer as younger, just waking up.)

What? What's the matter? What time is it?

(As mother) It's 2:00 A.M.. Come on you have to come with
Mumma. Grandma's having one of her spells again. We need to
get to Aunt Judy's. Come on.

(Still as mother. Flashback to Gram on couch.)

Mumma? Mumma, it's Belle. Mumma? Come on, Mumma, you
need to get up.

[sternly] Mumma!

Mumma come on now, you need to get up.

*(Mother waves her hand in front of Gram's face. She becomes
fearful.)*

Mumma? Mumma?!

(As performer in present time.)

When I was around twelve, and fifteen, and seventeen, my mom would be summoned in the middle of the night to go to one of my aunts' houses because my gram was having one of her "spells." My mom would wake me up to go with her. And during these times I remember opening my eyes and seeing the uncharacteristic fear in my mom's face.

(Cross quickly to SL—the aunt's house.)

We would drive quickly in the dark, get to my aunt's house, and there Gram would be, *(sees grandmother)* lying on the couch

stiff,

still,

paralyzed,

her jaw locked,

her eyes half open.

I remember watching my mother

try to coax,

cajole,

and command

her mother

back into her body.

But something inside Gram would just   go off...

and she would leave us,

leave us her cracking shell,

her dry limbs brittle

from droughts of loneliness,
family chaos,
and—at that time—
the death of four children.

Sometimes Gram would   moan
through her clenched teeth
(Performer enacts the following.)
and we would all rush over
leaning close
trying to hear,
all of us leaning over her,
my mom,   my three aunts,   and me,
all of us
leaning over
watching bits
and pieces of ourselves   breaking
in Gram's
distorted face.

We stood there,
witches
over an ancestral cauldron
trying and trying
to incantate ourselves
out of the fear
and familiarity
of that face.

(Back to present time. Performer gradually becomes confused and angry.)

She lay there
captive of a stingy
shaming
Catholic
god
who required that she be either
Virgin Mary
or Magdalene the repenting whore.
Unwilling or unable to embody either,

(Performer turns US and begins walking in a circle.)
Gram looked back on her options,
and decided instead   to turn to stone
like Sister Sara.

(Flashback to breakdown. Sitting and swaying in a circle.)
I... I can't, I can't, um, I.... no, I have to... Deb? Carole? Oh... I, um...

(Back to present.)
And the last faces I saw
on the way down
were the faces of others,
others who found comfort
in the splitting of selves.

It was finals day in my Interpersonal Communication course. The last group had just finished a thorough and sensitive presentation on gendered reactions to sexual assault. And in the middle of the ensuing discussion I noticed Karen [gesture

toward chair]—usually a very active student in discussion—
[cross to chair] was slumped in her chair with her head on her
desk. Her eyes were partially opened, extremely dilated, and
tears were running down her face into a puddle on the desk.

(Flashback.)

"Karen? Karen?"

(Present time.)

I couldn't rouse her. She was catatonic… stiff… brittle… a
stone of salt…

(Flashback as Mom)

Little, Little, come on, wake up. Grandma is having one of
her—

(Back to performer within the story.) I quickly dismissed class
and called for the secretary to call 911 and my friend Nancy
who worked at the Sexual Assault Center. I tried unsuccess-
fully to pry the Diet Coke can from Karen's rigid grip.

(Flashback as Mom)

Mumma? Mumma—

(Back to performer in story.) I gently placed my hand on
Karen's back. "It's O.K, Karen. It's O.K." Just then two male
paramedics came in, and from a completely catatonic state,
Karen went ballistic. *(Performer enacts the following as if it
is happening.)* She bolted upright slamming both of us against
the wall. And when we came down, she grabbed hold of me
pleading, "Don't let them—don't let them touch me, they're
bad! Please, please don't let them touch me!"

And out of this thirty-two year old woman's body,
Carrie emerged.
Carrie told me she was six years old
and would not go with the bad men.

I rode in the ambulance with Karen and over the course of the
next three hours, emerging from Karen was six-year-old Carrie,
sixteen-year-old Sara, a German speaking person, a woman
who played piano, and a few others who weren't around long
enough to leave their name.

Finally, a member of Karen's family showed up, and someone
drove me to my car.
I drove home,
my head spinning.
I thought, "Wow, from a performance standpoint,
this woman could switch from persona to persona
like nobody's business."
And then I thought... and then I thought,
"Wait. Um, *I* can switch from persona to persona...
like...
nobody's business."

Well,
the fall had already begun.
I spent the next two nights in fitful nightmares
about Karen
and the others
and me.

Carole my therapist kept trying to assure me

(Flashback to breakdown.)

(Back to present.) that what I had witnessed was Multiple
Personality Disorder

(Flashback to breakdown.)

(Back to present.) and that I was *worlds* away from that.

But her voice
kept getting farther
and farther away
as I drove around town in circles,
walked around my house in circles,
and ended up in the middle of our family room floor
swaying
and babbling
and falling
in circles.

Two friends found me, called Carole, medicated me, and put
me to bed.
I woke up two days later, hazy, alive, and euphoric.
I had fallen, finally fallen;
and I wasn't in a garbage can,
I hadn't turned to salt,
and I was doing   multiple persona   only in rehearsal.

A year later a tree of life appeared on my skin with two women
dancing, kicking, and falling. And they are me, and Mom, and

Gram and many many others. The roots flow through us like a corporeal conduit between the above and below, between still-ness and motion [begin to dance], between darkness and light.

And now,

when I move in clarity or chaos,

we women come together.

And on a very good day,

I can hear them singing

and see them dancing.

Analyzing "Tattoo Stories"

"Tattoo Stories: A Postscript to 'Skins'" emerged two years after repeated performances of "Skins." My experience and explication of the autobiographical performance process began to merge with my work in ethnographic fieldwork and performance informed by the rhetorical and performative turn in anthropology articulated by Victor Turner, Clifford Geertz, Dwight Conquergood, Kristin Langellier, and others.

I found the dynamic and dialectical relations of the text and body to be a major theme in autoethnographic praxes (Anzuldua 1995, Denzin 1992, Ellis and Bochner 1996, Goodall 2002). In the fieldwork, writing, and performing of autoethnography, text and body are redefined, their boundaries blurring dialectically. The researcher, in context, interacting with others becomes the subject of research, thereby blurring distinctions of personal and social, self and other (Conquergood 1991). Trinh Minh-ha writes, "Experience, discourse, and self-understanding collide against larger cultural assumptions concerning race, eth-nicity, nationality, gender, class, and age" (1991, 157). For me, plaiting ethnography with autobiography emphasizes the cul-tural situatedness of the autobiographic subject.

Autoethnographic texts reveal the fractures, sutures, and seams of the text's generation of self interacting with others in the context of researching lived experience. In interpreting the autoethnographic text, readers feel/sense the fractures in their own communicative lives, and, like Gramsci's notion of the organic intellectual, create efficacy and healing in their own communal lives. Barbara Jago writes of her autoethnographic work with family stories:

> Because we tell our stories within the frames of dominant cultural myths, the aspects of our experience we can include are limited. Once such myths are identified and externalized, people can begin to rewrite alternate life stories outside of the dominant cultural narrative, reselecting elements of their experience to support a new and more satisfying vantage point. (1996, 507)

Thirteen years after I was sexually assaulted, profound healing came when I began to rewrite that experience as a woman with strength and agency rather than accepting the victimage discourse of sexual assault embedded in our phallocentric language—and, thus, value—systems (Spry 1995).

As I continue to write and perform autoethnography, I believe I exist somewhere amid the sociopolitical narratives written on my body. My body is a cultural billboard advertising the effects of selves/others/contexts interacting with and upon it. Identity exists in a constant flux of interpreting self's interactions with others in sociohistorical contexts (Trinh 1991; Smith, "Performativity," 1998). Autoethnography—with its body in the borderlands of autobiography and ethnography—is a narration signifying at least one interpretation of ever-fluctuating identity. And since the autoethnographic story is a discursive act, it is always turning back upon itself, effecting a continual praxis of identity tangled in the reifications and resistances of other(ed) bodies in the body politic. The autoethnographic "I," then, becomes a plural pronoun with the constant refraction of selves in disparate locations (Smith, "Bodies," 1993.)

Performance presents another location as I/we constitute selves in the staged moment of performance. Working off Jacques Derrida's "law of genre," Caren Kaplan (1998) argues that this plural "I" constitutes an "out-law" genre in its resistance to master genres in autobiography. Out-law genres in autobiography reveal the "power dynamics embedded in literary production, distribution, and reception" (208). Kaplan maintains that these emerging out-law genres "are more closely attuned to the power differences among participants in the process of producing the text. Thus, instead of a discourse of individual authorship, we find a discourse of situation; a 'politics of location'" (208). The post-colonial ethnographic and performance theory imperative of contextualizing the subject and the subjective researcher creates a tight theoretical weave with Kaplan's discourse of situation.

Kaplan illuminates the epistemological processes that guide my work in autoethnography, specifically in "Tattoo Stories." Her focus on power dynamics in literary production, distribution, and reception is the theory link to my lived experience of generating, rehearsing, and debuting "Tattoo Stories" at the last Otis J. Aggert (OJA) Festival in 1996. Using the dancing/kicking/falling figures on my newly minted tattoo as a metaphor, this performed autoethnography monographed my experiences between sanity and mental illness. Before the OJA Festival, this particular all-too-lived-experience was not one I had shared with anyone but intimate friends. I felt like a madwoman debutante presenting my psychotic selves at the Performance Studies Society Ball. The people assembled at this festival are often faculty of prestige in performance studies, some of whom I know well, others who believe they know me well. This gathering was no different. As I constructed this performance, the dynamics of professional status and impression management caused weird collisions with the already personally and culturally fractured self created out of notes and memory of going mad. Here, the "distribution" and "reception" of the text is performance, and packed with power differences.

Kristin Langellier's recent writing on "performativity" helps me make further sense of these collisions in the performance of personal narratives, "Approaching personal narrative as performance requires theory which takes context as seriously as it does text, which takes the social relations of power as seriously as it does personal reflexivity, and which therefore examines the cultural production and reproduction of identities and experience" (1999, 128). The "social relations of power" in the *context* of that debut performance were as constitutive of the autoethnography's literary production as the personal relations of power entangled in my alliance with my mother articulated in the *content* of "Tattoo Stories."

And again, it is the verisimilitude of the "'un/learning body' crashing clumsily through paper and landing in a heap on the stage" (Madison 1999, 107) in performance that critically illuminates particular social relations of power between myself and an academic community. In "Dancing Bodies and the Stories They Tell," Ann Cooper Albright writes: "In performance, the audience is forced to deal directly with the history of that body in conjunction with the history of their own bodies. This face-to-face interaction is an infinitely more intense and uncomfortable experience which demands that the audience engage with their own cultural autobiographies" (1997, 121).

The verisimilitudinal stakes are vastly different when I perform "Tattoo Stories" for a Women's Center audience than when I perform this work for a scholarly convention audience. The meanings and desires of myself and the audience are terribly transformed due to the personal and professional expectations, ideologies, and politics inherent in these grossly different contexts. Albright continues, "Thinking of autobiography as a performance...helps us to keep the physical body in mind yet paradoxically refuses any essentialist notion of bodily experience as transparent and unmediated by culture" (120). Ethnographer Ruth Behar (1997) asserts that autoethnography brings the researcher "so disturbingly present" (25) to the audience, creating a context whereby meanings and interpretations are created between the participants in a flesh to flesh theorizing.

But theorizing "flesh to flesh" amidst the OJA audience brought to bear the histories of our flesh that, too ironically, contributed to the break(through)down described in "Tattoo Stories." Smith (1998) suggests that communal discourses and practices determine how the body is called together as a "unified or coherent material reality with specific identity constructions" ("Bodies" 128). The OJA audience represented for me a reified and hegemonizing communal narrative—a mini version of the wider communal narrative of academe, highly determinant in the "calling together" of the material body "with specific identity constructions."

Up until five years ago, my performance of self in academe was an exhausting artifice. Beginning with my first years in grad school I carefully observed the social constructions of "scholar" performed at academic conventions. I watched, listened, and sought to construct a believable version of "successful academic." As a woman, I gendered myself in a costume of heels, hose, suit, and power hair. I networked, performed intellectual-white-middle-class-liberal-feminist, and was wounded and inflicted wounds common in the competitive battlefield of the academy. I used my body as a billboard, advertising all of the insightful thoughts and attractive personal attributes required for full membership into the academic fraternity. I distorted my scholarly voice into a distanced, disembodied, phallocentric mimicry. I dissertated, published, tenure-tracked, nursed a dying mother, birthed a child, maintained a troubled marriage, and finally, inevitably, thankfully, had a mental breakdown. "Tattoo Stories" is the story of that breakdown. So, I would be debuting an autoethnographic performance in a context that helped cause the mental rupture described in the performance.

Strangely (or maybe quite ordinarily), performing that narrative in that context to that audience created for me a profound emancipation from the coherent material realities called together upon my body in a communal narrative of the academy. The performance was, for me, a "coming out ball." (Read within that phrase the [extra]ordinary mix of queer theory with bourgeoisie gender presentation; it was all part of the sociopolitical mix of identity construction I was experiencing.) Not only was I tearing off the skins of my mother 'in' performance, I was also breaking out of an academic communal narrative that I had long used as a corset restricting the breath and breadth of my personal/professional body. Furthermore, "Tattoo Stories" describes the experience of a "Hysterical Woman," a bodily experience grotesque to the Mind of the Academy. Smith writes, "The body categorized as abnormal becomes associated with those forces threatening the stability of the body politic. It becomes a pollutant, a grotesquerie" (128). Smith adds that while the autobiographical subject "finds herself subjected to the social meanings of bodies, she can find ways to resist the kind of body pressed upon her through the body politic" ("Bodies" 130). I cannot stop the modernist mediated profiles of identity scripted upon my body, but because identity exists amidst discursive profiles, I can change the way I dialogically engage these stories; for me, this change is most profound through performance.

Performing autoethnography has motivated an intense shift in the shape of my life. It has been a vehicle of resistance and emancipation from cultural and familial identity scripts that have governed the size and shape of my body and identity personally and professionally. The point of my work is to express scholarship in ways that mirror the passion, pain, and hope of lived experience. This work has literally saved my life by providing me the means to claim reflexive agency in my interactions with others in contexts. My body is still a cultural billboard, but its advertisements promote the "insightful thoughts and attractive personal attributes suggested for full membership" into a life of hope and renewal.

I began creating a self in and out of academe that allowed an expression of passion and spirit I had long suppressed. Although expressing passion and spirit within the communal narrative of academe seemed more like heresy than successful scholarly practice, in going mad, I had learned that heresy is greatly maligned and, when put to good use, can be the music that begins a robust dance of agency in one's personal/political/professional life.

"Skins" was about dancing and kicking.

"Tattoo Stories" is about falling through paper and landing in a heap on a bare stage.

As articulated in chapter 1, perhaps the most important facet of performative autoethnography is connection. In the opening of this chapter Gomez-Pena and bell hooks articulate two of the most defining features of performative autoethnography, its connection to larger social issues and to the commitment of well crafted writing. In "Tattoo Stories" and the analysis that accompanied it in 2000, I try to illustrate the process and product of these connections as they occur in critical self-reflection.

Performative autoethnography exists in the nexus of personal experience and larger social issues. The writing process seeks to articulate that space, that meeting place, that *intersection* that Gomez-Pena identifies where our personal experiences interconnect with social and cultural issues. A critical pedagogy exists in those personally political spaces between interruption and perpetuation of pain and injustice. It is a space of decision making. It is an autoethnographic space that presents an opportunity for intimate self revelation and evolution about how learned injustices affect behavior, and thereby presents a space for personal/political efficacy.

Certainly, our personal experience, our everyday life, is immersed in sociocultural contexts. There are, however, particular experiences in our lives that foreground these connections. Trinh writes, "Not every personal event is political, but all personal events certainly have the potential to be political. The personal politicized and the political personalized is the inbetween ground where the questioning work materializes itself" (1991, 113). That inbetween ground is the homespace of performative autoethnography. When analyzed through the performative autoethnographic process, those experiences become critical pedagogical studies that reveal our interconnectedness and the conflictual effects of the choices we make in perpetuating or challenging oppressive performances of race, gender, class, religion, etc.

Writing performative autoethnography is about developing one's relationship with words; it is about developing an acute awareness of the implications that language is the only thing we have between us to express the complexity of our thoughts and experience. In the earlier discussion of agency and representation, we established how autoethnographers must develop a sociopolitical awareness of the ways in which words represent and illustrate our values and beliefs, our view of self, others, and culture. The writing process is both catalyst for and illustration of agency and representation.

This chapter is about writing within the performative-I disposition; it is about putting the body on the paper; it is about what to consider in writing the textualizing body. Specifically, this chapter: 1) discusses performative writing or writing the performative body as embodied, coperformed, evocative, and consequential; 2) offers an ethic of aesthetics to guide the aesthetic/epistemic praxis in autoethnographic writing, arguing that the aesthetic writing/crafting of autoethnography, rather than considered merely a scholarly bonus, requires as much attention to its inherent political effects as does the writing/crafting of knowledge, and 3) furthers the development of the textualizing body.

Putting the Body On Paper, or, Writing the Performative Body

It may be becoming clear that words and the body are inseparable in performative autoethnographic writing. Words represent bodies, how bodies move, react, interact; words represent how bodies perform in their everyday lives. Our task in performative autoethnography is to make writing perform, to make writing represent the complexity of the body's critical expression of interacting with others in the frames of social norms and expectations, and then write the body's transformation of those norms. "In performative writing," writes Madison, "we recognize that the *body* writes. Critical ethnography adheres to radical empiricism: the intersection of bodies in motion and space" (2005, 195). Performative writing is the process of making writing perform "bodies in motion and space" on the page.

So, how to do this? Where to start? What to think?

As always, in performance, we start with the body and its engagement with words. In Ken Gale and Jonathan Wyatt's work "Writing the Incalculable," Gale writes, "When you write about feeling Janice inside you, you make literal the feelings that were seeping out of you and into your writing, staining the page, allowing the effects to make their mark" (2007, 797). A palpable example of performative writing, we can feel the body of the author on the page; we can feel him "staining the page" through embodied language; we can feel his relationship with words. We feel his experience. Here, rather than solely a tool to express knowledge, language is something created and creative in the action of writing, in the corporeal sensuousness of writing.

Performative writing composes the body into being. Such a praxis requires that I believe in language's representational abilities, thus putting my body at (the) stake (Spry 2001). I find the ability and desire to "sentence my way" (Pelias 2007, 192) through critical reflection where

I might feel a connection, a disposition, a figure of relation with others. Crafting language through performative writing is to engage in a call to constant disruption (of norms, narratives, nomenclature), creating and speaking into the crisis of representation.

Our Relationship with Language

Seeking to connect word and body does not always bring about agreement between the two. Critically reflecting upon one's experience with others is not always easy or comfortable. Engaging in a call to constant disruption of power structures and of our own biases means identifying and articulating how those power structures and biases are lodged in our bodies and in our everyday practices of living. For example, what is the effect on our *connection* to larger social issues with the (un)conscious use of words like "fag" or "bitch" and others that create a constant level of intolerance and judgment that add bricks to the walls between us. What is the connection between these words and our bodies, between these words and our everyday lives? Why do we use these words? What do we get out of it? Performative writing asks us to engage these questions rather than making a facile promise to ourselves and/or others to stop or to obstinently continue using these kinds of words. Performative writing in autoethnography asks us to critically reflect upon our relationship with words and then to try and tell a different story than taken-for-granted social assumptions. When done well, it pulls the rug out from under the boots of privilege (which can often be one's own), while simultaneously offering hands to grasp if and when we fall. The entangled body is the site from which language constructs the evocation of personal politics, of intimate global transformation, "staining the page" with critical imaginings of hope.

In thinking about developing our own relationship to words as well as the descriptors of performative writing that follow, consider the following excerpt from "Call It Swing":

How do we practice what Butler calls, a 'critique that exposes the limits of the historical scheme of things'(17)? How do we

begin a post 9-11 improvisation that includes the conditions
of our own emergence, with a language that is bloated with
histories of slavery and continued oppression, a language that
often does not swing, a language that produces and maintains
an 'n' word? A kind of word that gets caught in the throat like a
marble, preventing speech or song. Or its use accumulates in the
throat like shards of glass, cutting, tearing, mutilating, slashing
breath that comes in and words that go out. Maybe what we
need is a language *interrupted* with empathy and compassion,
with a jazz swing, with truth and reconciliation.

Some months ago, while working on this piece, I was talking with a student from Kenya. We were talking about Barak
Obama and I mentioned how hungry people are in the U.S. for
a discourse of compassion. And she said, 'Are you sure?' she said,
'because you Americans are so used to being insulted by one
another, your television, your media, your language,' she said
'Africans just don't talk to one another that way.' I'm not trying
to make a culturally essentializing observation about Americans
and Africans and all of the power differentials at work in that
exchange, rather, that exchange was an interruption of language
for me, an interruption of the European Waltz of language, an
engagement of deep swing. And my heart began to ache thinking of how numbed we are to the banal meanness of our cultural
scripts. Her observation created, a breech, a threshold, a space
where through a performative ethos and critical imagination,
we might consider hope not as an escape for the naive, but as
something with powerful compassionate potential.

Scholarships interrupted by critical imaginings of hope are
transgressive scholarships of the body with a heart. It is D. Soyini
Madison's *Acts of Activism*, Dwight Conquergood's people's
ethic of dialogical performance, and the roaming free radical
Norman K. Denzin's radical critical performance pedagogy of
hope. And most importantly, it is a language made and remade,
interrupted, and continually reconstructed by us as we trip and

stumble over the language of one another's bodies, and then help one another up, sometimes in anger, sometimes with compassion, but always with hearts full of new words that might dislodge a marble, or gingerly pick out the shards of glass, trying not to get cut. (276–277)

Autoethnography Descriptives

Performance studies scholars Della Pollock, D. Soyini Madison, and Ronald Pelias have offered descriptives of this kind of scholarly writing that "stain the page" or "might dislodge a marble." Performative writing foregrounds our development of a relationship to words and language. Though each of these scholars offers varying and cogent terms, each contends that writing must *perform* on the page. Performative autoethnographic writing seeks to put the body's critical creative interpretation of self/other/culture on the page. In her ground breaking work "Performing Writing," Pollock (1998) articulates writing as evocative, subjective, nervous, citational, and consequential. In Madison's (2005) foundational work in performance ethnography, she describes writing as relational, evocative, embodied, consequential. And in his influential work on performative writing, Pelias explains writing as embodied, evocative, partial, material (2007). These descriptors embody the rich complexity of autoethnographic writing, and surely our discussions thus far reflect their influence. With these descriptors as guides we will focus on performative autoethnography then, as embodied, coperformed, evocative, and consequential.

In conceptualizing writing as embodied, Pollock argues, "It [performative writing] requires that the writer drop down to a place where words and the world intersect in active interpretation, where each pushes, cajoles, entrances the other into alternative formation, where words press into and are deeply impressed by "the sensuousness of their referents'" (1998, 81). Intersection of words and bodies, "staining the page," "intersect[ing] in active interpretation," viewing language as embodied and performative foregrounds the process involved in the embodied doing of language in performative auto-ethnography. Notice in the above excerpt on "an 'n' word" how the body is implicated in forming the word, it gets "caught like a marble" in the throat, or its use accumulates in the throat like "shards of glass." My intention was to generate a coperformed meaning with the reader/audience about how racism's language *feels* in the body; I want to create a collaborative embodied experience with the audience through the writing performing on the page.

Performative writing is *coperformed* in its negotiations with others in contexts to illustrate our conflictual or differing experiences of power and privilege. In conceptualizing the writing in "Call It Swing" as coperformative, I look at the ways in which race relations between my dad and other musicians is created in their relationship to one another in a particular sociocultural context. How did they experience race together interactively, or in other words, how did they perform race? And then, in looking at making meaning with my dad as coperformative, how did he communicate race in his everyday life as my father? This perspective offers a more complex process of engaging difficult social issues on the page.

Performative autoethnography is *evocative* in its insistence upon an intimate articulation of what the body feels and knows in engagements with others, a felt-sensing, as Wallace Bacon would say, of reactions and interactions. The extensive work of Ellis and Bochner advocates the evocation of emotion in articulating meaning. Jonathan Wyatt writing to Ken Gale exemplifies an evocative felt sensing: "She was only in my head. I did not feel her. Last week I felt her inside me, in my stomach, in my chest, in my lungs and throat" (2008, 795). The body is evoked on the page.

Performative writing is surely *consequential* since critical reflection upon our own challenging and/or perpetuation of power is transformative. It is not innocent. Putting the body on the line in meaning making has consequences to ourselves and those around us. As Denzin mentioned in our introductory chapter, "Our research practices are performative, pedagogical, and political. Through our

writing and our talk, we enact the worlds we study. These performances are messy and pedagogical. They instruct our readers about
this world and how we see it" (2006a, 422). Performative writing can
be messy in that others will not see the world in the ways you write it.
Critically reflecting on oppressive sociocultural norms and expectations will certainly bring about disagreement and discomfort, which
will hopefully be the catalyst for substantive discussion about being
a citizen in the world. "Performative writing," asserts Pollock, "is an
important, dangerous, and difficult intervention into routine representations of social/performative life" (1998, 75).

If words are our means of expressing the complexity of being
human, then analyzing the aesthetics of writing are tantamount to
the check and balance of agency and representation. "Performative
writing," writes Pollock, "collapses distinctions by which creative
and critical writing are typically isolated" (80). In performative autoethnography the critical and creative work together. Words and body
are a praxis reflected through language, thus the aesthetic construction of language is part and parcel of this method of scholarship.

An Ethic of Aesthetics in Performative Autoethnography

*In the case of autoethnography, the two strands of barbed
wire manifest as a demand to create knowledge (the epistemic) and a demand to create art (the aesthetic). While
we need not see these demands as diametrically opposed,
neither need we see them as synonymous. In any event,
we leave the relationship between them unconsidered at
our peril.*

Craig Gingrich-Philbrook, *Autoethnography's Family
Values: Easy Access to Compulsory Experiences,* 303

Performative autoethnography is a critical moral discourse
(Conquergood 1985, 1991; Denzin 2003, 2008; Jones 2005). It
is grounded in "the performance paradigm [which] privileges

particular, participatory, dynamic, intimate, precarious, embodied experience grounded in historical process, contingency, and ideology" (Conquergood 1991, 187). Consequently, in autoethnography's trajectory and development as a moral discourse it must be, at its foundation, epistemic (creative of knowledge). *All of the potentials and possibilities embodied in performative autoethnography depend upon the quality of its report, of its linguistic and aesthetic construction, of it its ability to make writing perform* (Alexander 2006; Denzin 2002, 2006b; Gingrich-Philbrook 2001, 2005; Goodall 2001, 2008; Hamera 2006; Pelias 2005; Pollock 1998; Spry 2008, 2009; Trinh 1991). In others words, the quality of the writing, the aesthetics, is directly related to the quality of the scholarship epistemologically and heuristically, and its potential to be pedagogical. The moral imperative, then, of autoethnography is as much situated in its aesthetic craft as in its epistemological potential. The depth of knowledge generated (epistemology) by performative autoethnography is directly related to its aesthetic acumen; and just as autoethnography is a critical moral discourse, the aesthetic crafting of autoethnography is a sociocultural and political action. "Performance exposes aesthetics' social work," writes Hamera, "as embodied, processual, rhetorical, and political and especially, as daily, as routine, a practice of everyday life" (2006, 47). Here performative autoethnography, the performative-I disposition, operates as a movement of epistemologically embodied art crafted within and between representations of power and powerlessness.

Performative autoethnography is writing from/with/of the coperformative body as copresent with others, the body as epistemologically central, heuristically inspirational, politically catalytic. Though performative autoethnography is a moral discourse, it does not seek to provide a "moral to the story." We write from within the entanglements of copresence, from the rapture of communion, from the un/comfortable risk and intimacy of dialogue, from the vulnerable and liminal inbetweeness of self/other/context.

Language of the Body

But it is, of course, *through language* that we body forth in interpreting and articulating what the body "knows." As mentioned earlier in "Bodies of/as Evidence," in postmodern research, we sometimes like to think of the body as inherently "knowing" things without remembering that *the body knows what language constructs* (Spry 2009). In conceptualizing performative writing, Craig Gingrich-Philbrook lives "in body-language-body-language. My body makes language. It makes language like hair" (2001, 3). Embodied knowledge is generated from a body-language rapture, elation, conflation, each affecting (and sometimes abjecting) the other.

Here is where the textualized body, as discussed in the introductory chapter, functions as a nexus in the conceiving and writing of autoethnography. Thinking about and writing about how your body performs in your everyday life is an interdependent process. For example, how do you "talk" about your body? When and why do you talk about it in positive terms or negative terms? How does this affect your self-concept? How does the way bodies are talked about in culture or the media affect your concept of others' bodies?

> Write a short description of the size or shape or color of your body. Look carefully at the language you chose. How is your choice of language affected by social expectations of body types?

The language we use to talk about or describe or refer to bodies governs how those bodies will be treated personally and politically. Language is inherently political, choosing language to critically reflect is a political and moral process. Thus we must take seriously the language chosen, its aesthetic crafting, when writing performative autoethnography.

The aesthetic crafting of language in autoethnography is an ethical imperative, *a movement of embodied art crafted within a performative-I disposition.* In a foundational article, "Autoethnography's Family Values: Easy Access to Compulsory Experiences," Gingrich-Philbrook (2005) deftly articulates the double bind of the aesthetic (the writing process) and the epistemic (articulation of knowledge) in autoethnography as a response, in part, to what he argues is a regulatory valuing and valorizing of emotionality in autoethnography at the expense of developing alternative theory and aesthetic practices in autoethnography. Simply writing emotion is not performative autoethnographic writing. Performance studies practitioners have worked with the embodiment of emotion in the production of knowledge for centuries, and are aware of the potential dangers when expecting the expression of emotion in research to stand-in for aesthetic acumen. Emotion is not inherently epistemic. I have tomes of writing expressing the emotional turmoil of loss during childbirth; as significant as that writing is to my own personal grief process, it is not performative autoethnography if it does not connect these emotions to larger social issues. Amanda's story is autoethnographic because she reflects upon social constructions of assault along with her emotional response to the assault. "Tattoo Stories" is autoethnographic due to its critical reflection on mental health. Hamera helps clarify:

> *Experience is not scholarship....* Performance links experience, theory, and the work of close critique in ways that make precise analytical claims about cultural production and consumption, and expose how both culture and our claims are themselves constructed things, products of hearts and souls, minds and hands. (2006, 241, emphasis mine)

Many aspects of my own personal grief are not yet critically reflective of how this experience is personally part of sociopolitics, of cultural production. The experience may surely be embodied, but is not yet performed on the page through language choice; it is not yet a textualizing body.

Aesthetic Accountability

Autoethnography fails if we look at the epistemic as more socio-politically and academically relevant, while viewing the aesthetic or literary as an added scholarly bonus, or worse, as ideologically benign. Gingrich-Philbrook employs the work of Murray Krieger who argues that the aesthetic "alerts us to the illusionary, the merely arbitrary claims to reality that authoritarian discourse would impose upon us; because, unlike authoritarian discourse, the aesthetic takes back the 'reality' it offers us in the very act of offering it to us" (quoted in Gingrich-Philbrook 2005, 310). Performative autoethnography is forged in the ontological tension between its epistemological potential and its aesthetic imperative. It is through language, afterall, that we "give an account of ourselves." Language's propensity toward imperializing, toward "merely arbitrary claims to reality," makes this accounting a moral commitment, an ethical imperative. Privileged people need not attend to imperializing aesthetics, as their words are framed by power. It is ethically imperative then, that the autoethnographer, who may certainly carry privilege into the research context, be acutely aware of the power dynamics involved in the aesthetics of performative autoethnography. Representation has risks (Denzin 2002, 2006a, 2008; Denzin et al. 2008; Grande 2008; Madison 2005, 2009; Poulos 2009; Smith 1999; Spry 2008). Aesthetics are not ideologically benign. Those risks can be negotiated by an ethic of care for aesthetic representation.

An ethic of aesthetic representation is illustrated through what Mindy Fenske calls an "ethic of answerability" where, in this case, the autoethnographer is responsible for and ethically liable for linguistic representations of the interpolations of self with others in contexts (2004, 8). Extending our concept of the textualizing body, Fenske argues that no hierarchy exists between craft and emotion, form and production, theory and practice, art and life. "Instead," she writes, "such relations are unified and dialogic....Art and life are connected, one is not meant to transcend the other. Both content and experience, form and production...exist inside the unified act in constant interaction" (9). In this dialogical ethic of care, emotion is not touted as the scholarly cure for realism, nor is aesthetic craft viewed as a mechanized technique handcuffing the raw essence of experience and emotion; rather they are interdependent upon one another, responsible to one another, liable to one another to represent the complex negotiations of meaning between selves and others in power laden social structures. *Here art is not a reflection of life, they are, rather, answerable to one another.* "Form," writes Fenske "becomes a location inciting, rather than foreclosing, dialogue" (11). The debilitating binary argument of craft over emotion, or practice over theory is deflated through Fenske's argument because these elements are mutually answerable to one another; knowledge is sought through their dialogic engagement suggesting a praxis, an ethical assembly, a resistance of hierarchy, a researching body dialogically engaging language. Rather than a linear path from self to other, theory to practice, or emotion to craft, performative-I disposition is a dialogic space where experience and text affect and are affected by one another in a textualizing body.

The Answerable Body

Clearly, embodiment is crucial in this ethics of aesthetics. Just as emotion and experience are not inherently epistemic, Fenske reminds us that "events are not ethical simply because they are embodied….In order to achieve answerability, the embodied action must be responsible for its meaning, as well as liable to meaning" (12). The material body cannot be erased in composing autoethnography, rather the corporeal body is made fully present in performance and represented through language that critically reflects upon the body's social constructions. In a recent student's performative autoethnography titled "Driving While Black," the truths of Anthony's life are not compromised by aesthetic craft; rather it is in the critical dialogic process of articulating, of crafting life that Anthony constructs and embodies knowledge that is subversive, pedagogical, and heuristic. Politically troubled aesthetics allow Anthony to read and re/write his social body as a transgressive text. To operate as if there is a hierarchy in art or life, in craft or emotion, in theory or practice is to engage, Fenske argues, "a type of aesthetic that lets the artist off the ethical hook" (13) by being tempted to offer simplistic notions of the "purity" (read apolitical) of embodied experience in aesthetic composition.

Any methodology, aesthetic or otherwise, that does not exercise as fundamental the critique of sociocultural systems and discourses of power sanitizes and imperializes critical reflexivity into a parlor game of identity construction where Self stands in front of a mirror trying on different cultural hats to see the "world" from the eyes of the Other. Autoethnography remains accountable by considering the political constructions of an "'I' that remains skeptical of authentic experience" (Jackson and Mazzei 2008, 314) and, I would argue, of aesthetic purity.

A few years ago I was on a panel with respected colleagues who were given the charge to discuss the future of autoethnography. I was just beginning to flesh out an argument for the ethics of craft in autoethnography since our methodological conversations at that point were centered upon the expression of emotion in research as a reaction to the dominant specter of objectivity and realist ethnographic methods. As I finished my remarks and sat down, a colleague, who had spoken right before me and who was seated next to me, stood up with grand attention, threw her arm in front of me and proclaimed, "I do not *do* craft!" Hmmm. Surely, I had not yet made my argument clear since I know this colleague's work to be well crafted and epistemic. Her further remarks conceptualized aesthetic craft as an imposed formalist act upon the uncorrupted expression of raw lived experience. As articulated by Conquergood 1991, 1998; Fenske 2004; Gingrich-Philbrook 2005; Hamera 2002, 2006, 2006a; Krieger 1962; Pollock 1998, and others, we ignore the politics embedded in craft at our peril. Gingrich-Philbrook:

> Autoethnography's emphasis on naïve critical realism—a faith in the absolute transfer of a commensurate account of an experience—over ambiguity, indeterminacy, and suggestion

reinscribes only the most dominant sense of 'poetry,' and that sense too easily devolves into triviality or 'inspirational verse' for my tastes. (2005, 308)

Hamera reminds us that "aesthetics is inherently social" (2006a, 46). Gingrich-Philbrook agrees, "Krieger maintains that he 'came to understand the extent to which the artistic medium—language in the specific case of literary art—together with the convictions that become attached to it over the centuries, generates a resistance to the intentions that the artist thought he or she had going into the process'" (2005, 309). Considering critical aesthetics, hooks writes, "It becomes ruthlessly apparent that unless we are able to speak and write in different voices, using a variety of styles and forms, allowing the work to change and be changed by specific settings, there is no way to converse across borders, to speak to and with diverse communities" (1999, 41). I believe the colleague I refer to and most others would agree with hooks's statement; it is in the proclamation of *doing* craft, the performativity of craft, that autoethnography assists in the diversity of transgressive narratives. As quoted at the top of this chapter, "Every woman's confessional narrative," writes hooks, "has more meaningful power of voice when it is well crafted" (1999, 68); and, I would add, when the researcher's body is viewed as in dialogue with language construction.

Performance, which at its heart is the embodiment of language, has also taught me a skepticism of language's ability to represent me or others outside of the dominant master narratives that it is meant to serve. This skepticism of language's ability to represent the body as evidence motivates the critical reflection upon the systems of power held in place through language. Kreiger writes, aesthetics

allows us an awareness of existence that enriches, as it softens, our humanity. In the everyday world of action, of decision-making, literature, unlike any other discourse, does not help us to decide so much as it warns us to distrust the decisions we must make. When we are required to choose one path rather than another, it reminds us to tread with a light foot and a heavy heart. (1962, 261)

Kreiger's "warning" is in a sense the essence of the counterbalance between agency and representation. I must always be wary of decisions made in representing others, cultures, myself. And this wariness, this awareness, this skepticism in turn may soften our human being. A continuous skepticism constitutes an ethical step into a consideration of an ethics of aesthetics in performative auto-ethnography. If I am continuously skeptical of language's ability to represent, to make meaning, to create reality, then I am located within a constant copresence with others questioning issues of culture and power embedded in the performativity, or the *doing,* of language.

Making writing perform. Making the story answerable to its own sociocultural emergence, to its own performance, to its own life as art and back again. Pelias writes, "Language is my most telling friend, my most fierce foe...power lurks, will grab me at every turn. I must stare it down, write it down" (2007, 193). Power lurks as much in aesthetic construction as in epistemological construction because surely, they are inseparable. And though they are answerable to one another, the answers do not foreclose one another. Performative autoethnographic writing is about the continual questioning, the naming and renaming and unnaming of experience through craft, through heart, through the textualizing body.

> Think of an instance where you are skeptical of language. Write a paragraph describing when, where, why.

Performative autoethnography is a moral discourse with ethical imperatives. It is creative and critical, empowering and accountable, and is written as collaborative with others in contexts. All of these theoretic frames, however, are made significant only through the act, the process, the commitment to language and writing. The danger of a single story is addressed by writing another, communicating another story of a cultural performative.

Now. It's time to write.

Questions for Further Consideration

1. What is the relationship between language and the body in writing performative autoethnography?

2. Choose any of the performative autoethnography examples in the book thus far ("Skins," "Tattoo Stories," "Call It Swing") and give an example of each of the descriptors of performative writing as embodied, coperformed, evocative, and consequential.

3. How is representation of others engaged ethically in the aesthetic/epistemic praxis?

4. How and why is the aesthetic craft of writing political?

Chapter Three

Paper
Composing Performative Autoethnography

Writing Bodies into Being

Placing oneself level with the body in writing, is, among other things, putting one's finger on the obvious, on difference, on prohibition, on life.

Trinh T. Minh-ha, *When The Moon Waxes Red*, 131

Katrina: A Jazz Standard

Seven days

Seven days after

Seven days after   on the Today Show

Seven days after   on the Today Show

Wynton Marsalis

wails

standing alone with his horn

standing,   delivering,   wailing

for Katrina
the blue swing sounds from his horn
rippling like water against a rooftop.

Seven days after
Wynton Marsalis
wails
reminding us
that this is no different
Katrina
is no different
no different
from centuries of reasons
for the blues

this treatment of people
this coda of color
a blues refrain
a jazz standard.

Wynton Marsalis plays
in the wake
of news clips and sound bites
of Katrina's people
a stream of jazz consciousness
a blues riff circa 1640 and beyond
with bodies of blues
piled into

the bellies of boats.

West Africa Ireland   West Indies   South America

Now,
New Orleans,
no boats come for those born of the 1640s,
no food or water for Katrina's people,
strong bodies reaching, holding,
tending, lifting, crying,
floating, dying,
surviving,
living.

Wynton's is not the song
of the president who stands on drowned earth
patting his FEMA buddy's body on the back
Those bodies would have been scooped up
before the first refrain.

Listen.

wails Wynton's horn,
no shock and awe here,
we know this song.

The blues is about telling people where you are now,
and jazz is about improvising where you want to be,
improvising desire.

"The notes," writes Wynton
"are merely the covering, the façade.
Listen to what they express. Then you will hear meaning" (ix).
Bodies reaching, holding, lifting
breaking and remaking
Katrina into a
jazz standard.
"To play jazz," says Wynton, "you have to embrace swing.
Call it democracy and coordination under the duress of time,
or call it swing."

When I listen to the jazz swing of hope and desire,
I hear Wynton improvising a critical pedagogy of
hope and liberation and freedom and love,
to riff off a phrase of Norm Denzin's.
A transgressive song
in dissonance
with a political parable of malice and greed and thirst for
treasure.
A new old song,
a minor chord rewriting a major one,
a new language,
a post 9/11 improvisation,
Katrina   a new   jazz standard.

As discussed in chapter 2 and illustrated here in "Katrina,"
autoethnography is embodied, coperformed, evocative, and

consequential. We write from the body in relation to others in culture evoking critical reflection upon the personally political. And when we place ourselves, as Trinh (1991) says, "level with the body in writing," there are consequences…for the writer, for the audience, for scholarship. But, of course none of this can be realized until we begin writing.

So we will begin the writing process by using the Elements for Composing Performative Autoethnography explicated in this chapter. This composition method emerged from "placing [myself] level with the body" in my own practice over the last fifteen years, and through much of my writing from and to a culture of loss. The autoethnographic performance "Paper and Skin: Bodies of Loss and Life" was composed using this method and helped me make the choice to live. It brought my body back into being, brought me back into this world through "a carnivale of lost and found" (Spry 2006, 359).

The most successful writers of both fiction and non-fiction readily and heartily admit that writing is scary and intimidating (LaMott 1995). I did not enter academia wanting to write. I entered as a performer, believing as we do in performance studies, that the embodiment of literature is the most powerful form of transmitting knowledge. And surely, as an artist scholar of performance studies, I still believe that. However, the epistemological value of writing scholarship that challenged the restrictive model of traditional academic writing—writing that valued "the mind" over embodied knowledge and discourse—became essential to my personal and professional life (Spry 1997, 2001, 2004). Though I surely risk hyperbole by saying so, writing saved my life:

- ☞ "Ode to the Absent Phallus" gave me back the power I felt I had lost in being sexually assaulted; a power gained by articulating how my experience could uncover some systemic processes perpetuating a culture of rape.

- ☞ "Skins: a Daughter's Reconstruction of Cancer" helped me understand issues of gender identity and grief through reflecting upon my mother's death.

☞ "Tattoo Stories: A Postscript to 'Skins'" helped me make a mental break*through* out of a mental break*down*.

☞ "Call It Swing" moved me through the articulation of white privilege in reflecting upon my dad's life as a big band jazz drummer in the 30s and 40s.

And though I have mentioned through pseudonym only a few students whose work interrupted oppressive norms of gender, race, and sexual identities, my own life and the lives of my students have been changed, challenged, and enriched through the personally political wisdom articulated in the autoethnography performance studies classroom.

This is why we do performative autoethnography.

Beginning performative autoethnography means beginning a continual critically reflective movement through one's everydayness. It means engaging a performative-I disposition where we enhance our awareness of how our choices have conflictual effects upon ourselves and those around us. William, for example, becomes harshly aware of how his body as a gay man is "read" by others in a church or other religious contexts. He becomes aware of how the single story of homophobia situates him in relation to others in religious contexts and how his sexual identity affects and restricts his access into some religious social systems. Moving into a performative-I disposition allows Amanda to see the ways in which she is encouraged or expected to be silent and invisible as a sexual assault survivor, and how this silence in turn perpetuates a culture that sees less need for social services that assist and advocate for assault survivors. Anthony begins to articulate the sociopolitical mechanics of his black male body so often profiled as criminal behind the wheel of a car.

Living this kind of critical life in a performative-I disposition, as a writer of autoethnography, may seem for a time uncomfortable and disconcerting. Opening up to the ways in which we are all connected to one another causes us to become aware of our own social conditioning and a system of power relations that we are part of due to race, gender, size, etc., and which causes us to experience the world differently. As well as ourselves, this kind of critical perspective may make others uncomfortable. Men, for example, working within a performative-I disposition may become less tolerant of their peers who rely on the ease of using language denigrative of women. White people, for instance, are often unnerved talking about race, and may exert social pressure upon other whites who begin to call into question their own racial privilege. In this excerpt from "From Goldilocks to Dreadlocks: Hair-raising Tales of Racializing Bodies," I critically reflect upon my white boyfriend's reaction when he "found out" I had dated a Black man; though this is a nearly verbatim record of the conversation, my use here of the terroristic word "nigger" is carefully considered and used to deconstruct rather than perpetuate its use:

He had driven us out into the country. I had no idea where we were. I kept asking, "What's the matter?" Rigid silence.

Finally, still looking straight ahead, he said, "Did you fuck a nigger?"

I froze.

"Did you? Did you fuck a nigger?" He was rigid, compressed.

I stuttered. "What? Why?"

"Oh, God. You bitch." He looks at me. "Why the fuck didn't you ever tell me?"

"Wha-...it...it was before I knew you."

I was ashamed. Somehow he had shamed me.

Instantly, it became White Inquisition time, a test of my true whiteness. Many whites know this space. It is one of the racially shrouded places where we perpetuate our feelings of privilege. If any of us begin "mixing" with "others," this is the place where we reprimand one another for not performing our whiteness appropriately. This is the place where we *remind* each other who we really are. We hear things like, "It's OK to be friendly with them, but don't get too close," and "They may be friendly to your face, but they are very different when they're with their own kind." White women are particularly targeted for racial interrogations by white men. Whether I had "fucked" a "nigger" or not was not a concern over our relationship. Frank was trying to establish whether his trophy date had committed treason.

"Why the FUCK didn't you tell me?!"

as if were his due,

as if were his right,

no,

his *responsibility,*

to reproach

and condemn me

for misusing my racial status.

And in spite of myself,

I felt like a little girl who was in trouble. (60)

This performative autoethnography opens up candid discussions about taken-for-granted racism practiced by whites daily. Long held familial and societal beliefs are brought into relief and (re)considered. Though everyday life may become more complicated when embracing a performative-I disposition, it can also become more fully, passionately, and intensely engaged when connecting into the creative, critical, and cultural negotiations of meaning with others.

What To Write About?

In this book we have encountered many examples of what I and others have chosen to write about. In a sense, these mean nothing when considering what *you* might write about. Performative autoethnography is about your connection to others in contexts, and only you can decide what experiences are ready to be engaged through this method. To begin, focus on an experience—or a series of experiences—that changed your life in some way, or that was somehow transformative in terms of how you think, act, or see the world. The experience caused you to think/act/react differently than before its occurrence. In *Writing the New Ethnography*, H. L. Goodall suggests considering "your life as a *historical* artifact. What are the historical events that hold special meanings for you? Which ones have shaped your worldview?... *What makes you tick?* Or put differently, what is it that you live for: Who do you live for?" (2008, 143–144). Your answers to these questions may spark experiences in your life that will be the catalyst for critical reflection upon larger social issues.

The experience may have been *based on one particular event* such as a parent's—or one's own—divorce, an achievement such as graduation or sport event, a particular incident of racism or sexism where you were the recipient or perpetrator. However, the transformative experience may have been *a series of smaller or gradual events* that had its effect over a period of time. "Katrina," for example, was written two weeks after the storm and was the result of my engaging stories and news accounts over a period of time; but its commentary on race is something that I have thought and written about for many years.

There is no particular definition or profile of transformative events/experiences that is a catalyst for performative autoethnography; we are all transformed by various things based on our own experiences and sociocultural make-ups. Ultimately, it is an encounter or a number of encounters where one's life intersected with larger social issues, like the examples in this book.

Do not be discouraged if an experience does not readily come to mind. Remember that this kind of critical self-reflection most likely has not been a part of everyday meaning making strategies. It may take some time to realize the ways in which your experience has collided with, interrupted, or embraced larger social issues. For example, maybe critical reflection upon religion is traced through years of attending church, mosque, or synagogue; the critique is understood over a long period of time and involvement.

Vulnerability and Self-Disclosure

Though in performative autoethnography we engage the personal as a vehicle for understanding the socio-political, your carefully crafted and considered story is not about self-disclosure; self-disclosure is not, in itself, scholarship. Rather, your autoethnographic scholarship is an opening into the complex negotiations of meaning making with others for the purpose of adding alternatives to the single story; all personal experience is in concert with the political. You will know when it is time to begin making sense of a confusing or complex experience. You will know when it is time to tell the story.

There will always, however, be a degree of reticence in disclosing something about ourselves that others would not ordinarily know. But remember that you are the *agent*, the teller of your story, and as such, you have the agency, the power, the right, as well as, of course, the ethical responsibility to tell it. Remember why you are telling this story. Butler (2005) helps:

> There is a certain departure from the human that takes place in order to start the process of remaking the human. I may feel that without some recognizability I cannot live. But I may also feel that the terms by which I can be recognized make life unlivable. This is the juncture from which critique emerges, where critique is understood as an interrogation of the terms by which life is constrained in order to open up the possibility of different modes of living. (3–4)

Your work may open up "different modes of living" for others who may not have lived your experience, or if they have, so that they might engage your story as a catalyst for their own explorations.

As you will know when it is time to tell the story, you will also know when it is NOT time. Fiction author Grace Paley wrote, "There is a long time in me between the knowing and the telling" (1974, 127). Some significant or transformative experiences in our lives need more gestation time than others. I did not, could not, write about my mother's death until seven years after. I did not write about being sexually assaulted for over a decade after the fact. On the other hand, I began writing immediately—could not stop myself—after losing our child. All situations are different and deserve a great deal of consideration. There is a big difference in feeling fear of being *exposed* and feeling nervous about writing/performing autoethnography. If you feel like you want to share your story, your scholarship, with others, it may be time to do so. Listen to yourself.

Audience: Who Are We Writing To?

As mentioned earlier, performative autoethnography is about connection; it is about our connections to one another personally, socially, historically. We are, in a sense, writing to one another about these connections, and about the pain of disconnection. In critically reflecting on who we are and how we are connected to one another in the world, our intention is to give an account of ourselves to one another. In "Tattoo Stories" I try to articulate my connection with my mother while at the same time trying to account for issues of gender and mental health, my hope being that the performative autoethnography is a catalyst for audience members to reflect upon their lives with others.

The performative-I disposition in writing is built on the ethical check and balance of agency and representation. Agency refers to the empowerment and development of the author through critical reflection. Representation, how the author chooses to represent others in writing, constitutes an ethical responsibility to the audience. This ethical disposition assumes the immanent value of the reader/audience, and that the author is responsible for his aesthetic and epistemic actions. The writer's relationship with the audience is located, as Conquergood (1985) contends, in dialogic performance where self and other challenge and embrace one another; they give one another the respect of offering an account of themselves.

Notice, then, that our aim is not to persuade but to engage in collaborative meaning-making with the audience. In the previous passage from "Goldilocks," for example, my aim is not to *persuade* my audience that racism exists and must be eradicated. Rather my intention is that through dialogically engaging the performance, audience members might be able to put themselves in the place of me and/or Frank and thus be able to critically reflect upon their own choices in race matters. In other words, the autoethnographer wants her work to be *generative* personally, politically, pedagogically. We want an audience to be able to generate meaning in their own lives from listening and feeling into the aesthetic/epistemic process. Bryant Alexander explains "generative autobiography" as an empathetic connection that "links the performer and the audience in a larger socio-political context of sharing and shaping meaning" (2000, 103). I want the audience to shape their own meanings about race through empathetically connecting with the performative autoethnography.

Novelist David Foster Wallace suggests that "all the attention and engagement and work you need to get from the reader can't be for your benefit; it's got to be for hers" (quoted in Max 2009, 48). It is the intentional and critically reflexive connection of this narrative to larger social issues, to the politics, pleasure, and pain of other people, that distinguishes performative autoethnography as a methodology grounded in forging knowledge with others to dismantle and transform hegemonic performativities.

Methodology for Composing Performative Autoethnography

All of the elements within the methodology require critical reflection upon our engagement with others in culture, or the social conditions of our emergence and existence in various cultural systems like race, class, gender, etc. The methodology is derived from the performative-I disposition where we write from the inbetweeness of self/other/culture/language in "the push and pull between and among analysis and evocation, personal experience and larger social, cultural, and political concerns," as Jones writes of autoethnography (2008, 374). *The composition elements include 1) sociocultural context, 2) critical self-reflection, 3) self-other interaction, 4) the body, and 5) ethics.* They are a conflation of one another, meaning that they result in a story illustrating the blending of bodies, a continual open-ended conversation between the elements that create an argument, a critical reflection upon one's negotiations with others in contexts, in other words, a textual embodiment of the performative-I disposition, the textualizing body.

Similar to Kenneth Burke's dramatistic pentad (1989), these five elements in composing performative autoethnography are not discrete, but are interdependent upon one another. The writing of one will necessarily change the writing of another. Some elements will emerge as more relevant than others; they are not expected to be written in equal ratio; rather they are expected to play with and off one another dialectically. In "Red Pedagogy: The Un-methodology," Sandy Grande illustrates this kind of methodological movement in working with/in indigenous research methods; she writes, "My research is about ideas in motion. That is, ideas as they come alive within and through people(s), communities, events, texts, policies, institutions, artistic expression, ceremonies, and rituals" (2008, 233).

This writing method is not linear, but rather circular, back-and-forth, fragmented. You may start with the composition element of sociocultural context, jump to body, then to critical self-reflection, and back again. The ideas of your experience will come alive through writing as Grande suggests. As we begin, remember Gail Sher's "Four Noble Truths for Writers":

1. Writers write

2. Writing is a process

3. You don't know what your writing will be until the end of the process.

4. If writing is your practice, *the only way to fail is to not write.* (1999, 5, emphasis mine)

Sociocultural Context

Identify and describe the sociocultural norms and expectations of the cultural context in which your story/experience takes place.

☞ What are the expectations or norms, or the "single stories" about gender, religion, success, etc. that impact your performance of self within the experience? For example, after the initial police interview, it was two years before I told anyone about being sexually assaulted. The social expectation of the time was that it was somehow the "victim's fault" that she was assaulted. How, then, was I affected by that dominant social norm or narrative, that single story, and how do I want to critique it in relation to my experience?

☞ Identify and research the power systems at work in the sociocultural contexts in which your experience takes place.

☞ What are the social hierarchies and power relations involved, i.e., class, gender, race, religion?

☞ What kinds of cultural stereotypes hold these hierarchies in place? What are the dominant or master narratives at work in the sociocultural context? For example, in "Tattoo Stories," a dominant narrative that I grew up with was that only weak minded people needed therapy; I should just "buck up" and stop

> What are the social hierarchies or systems of power in your classroom? What are the expectations of class or financial status? of religion? of gender? of age?

being sad and upset; I should be ashamed of seeking therapy; or as in "From Goldilocks to Dreadlocks," interracial relationships were talked about as "jungle fever" rather than a serious relationship.

☞ What values and beliefs are illustrated through these norms and expectations?

  ☞ For example, what cultural values are illustrated through the difference in pay between a baseball star (Joe Mauer's $23 million a year salary) and an excellent public school teacher (average $35,000 a year)?

  ☞ How do these cultural values figure into your experience?

☞ What are the major critiques of these systems of power and/ or dominant narratives? What holds them in place? What cultural values, for example, would hold these dominant narratives in place?

☞ Focus the research:

  ☞ Social constructions of gender, race, etc. do not have distinct boundaries. The social expectations and norms that are created within these contexts are systemically played out in myriad ways *and are different for each person within the context.*

  ☞ Like any other research process, the autoethnographer must narrow the focus of the study. For example, Amanda's experience of sexual assault takes place in the sociocultural context of a suburban high school; she chose to focus on gender systems and identities as they were played out by her peers in that context.

Critical Self-Reflection

An autoethnography is first and foremost a *critical reflection* upon one's experiences within specific social/cultural/political locations.

This is the core of the performative-I disposition as described in chapters 1 and 2. There will necessarily be overlap between this element and the element of sociocultural context since critiquing self is inherently interwoven with one's social conditions. Critical self-reflection involves examining one's social/cultural/political *standpoint* within the context.

- What are the social hierarchies and power relations involved, i.e., class, gender, race, religion as analyzed in sociocultural context?

- *Where am I situated* within these structures? Why?

  - What is my relationship to constructions of class, gender, race, religion, etc. existing in these power structures? For example, how has my upbringing situated me in these structures?

  - Am I a cultural insider? Outsider? What effect does this have on my critique?

- How do the norms and expectations identified in sociocultural context affect me, i.e. self image, behaviors, the choices made?

  - How do I meet or not meet these expectations?

  - What are the consequences of my choices in meeting or not meeting these expectations, i.e. being judged by or rejected from peers, family, job?

  - How have these judgments or rejections been communicated to me?

  - Or, how have I been rewarded for meeting these expectations? For example, a woman who meets the cultural expectations of beauty is rewarded with attention and validation. What is the cost of this validation to herself and others? What cultural values about race, gender, etc. are being perpetuated by this validation?

☞ How do the norms and expectations identified in sociocultural context affect *others* in these structures?

  ▷ How do I believe others meet or do not meet these expectations?

  ▷ What are the consequences of their choices in meeting or not meeting these expectations, i.e. being rejected by peers, family, job?

  ▷ Compare and contrast the similarities and differences in consequences between you and others.

☞ When and where do I feel agency in these sociocultural contexts? Lack of agency? How is agency or lack of it connected to these power systems?

> When/how do you feel agency in this class? Why? When/how do you not feel agency in this class? Why?

☞ Where and when do I have cultural privilege? Lack of privilege? How is privilege or lack of it connected to these power systems?

  ▷ How does my racial, gender, religious, etc. privilege affect others within this autoethnographic experience?

  ▷ When/how have I used this to oppress another? Was it conscious? Did I know it at the time?

  ▷ How does my lack of racial, gender, religious, etc. privilege affect others within this autoethnographic experience?

  ▷ When/how have I experienced oppression or mistreatment due to a lack of privilege? Was it conscious/purposeful on the part of the other?

How does critically reflecting upon these sociocultural norms and expectations *change* your image, behaviors, and choices?

What are my motivations for writing this story? Why do I want to write this story?

Self-Other Interaction

This element focuses on the coperformativity of meaning making in performative autoethnography. Understanding that self is constructed through interactions with others, reflect upon and describe interactions that seemed significant within the scope of your experience. How does/can our engagement with others make or break normalized social expectations and/or dominant cultural narratives?

What interactions most affected your experience? Why?

How did these interactions challenge or perpetuate sociocultural norms or expectations of you or others?

How were these interactions affected by your own perceived sociocultural norms and expectations?

How were the interactions affected by privilege of class, race, gender, etc., that you may carry into the interaction?

How were they affected by a lack of privilege?

Does the person you interacted with have privilege or not? How did this affect interaction?

What interactions gained more meaning for you upon later reflection? Why?

Identify and describe patterns of words, language use, slang, phrases, or conversations that emerged in interactions with others.

What cultural symbolic value do they hold?

What is their sociocultural function? Is this function different in interactions between different people?

☞ Do you have cultural license to use these words? Why or why not?

The Body

This element focuses on embodiment, representation, and the relationship between the word and the body. Pineau writes, "From the moment of birth, cultural associations regarding ethnicity, class, gender, sexual orientation, able-bodiedness, and so on, are imprinted into our very musculature—these social norms shape our posture, measure our movements, inflect our voices, and pattern the ways we touch, experience, and interact with the bodies of others" (2002, 44). One's material body (color, gender, size, shape, etc.) and how that body interacts and reacts to the people and sociocultural context of the experience are critically reflected upon and *represented* through autoethnography.

☞ How is your body "read" within the sociocultural context of the experience?

☞ Does the color, gender, size, shape, clothing of your body meet or differ from cultural norms and dominant narratives operating within the sociocultural context?

☞ Does your body offer you privilege? Subjugation? How? Why?

  ☞ Does this change with different groups of people? How?

☞ When and how do you fulfill or purposefully work against the readings or cultural expectations of your body?

  ☞ Why? In what situations/contexts?

  ☞ When is it to your advantage? Disadvantage?

☞ What does your body "feel" or felt-sense in relation to interactions with others?

  ☞ Comfortable? Empowered? Objectified? How? Why? A mix of both depending on whom you are interacting with?

- ☑ When and where and with whom does this change?

- ☑ Describe physical reactions due to the experience you are describing.

  - ☑ Was there illness involved? Does your experience deal with surviving an illness and becoming healthy/healed, or not?

  - ☑ Were there particular physical occurrences that were significant to your experience? For example, how does a mastectomy affect a woman's perception of herself, others' perceptions of her? What are the politics of reconstructive surgery?

- ☑ Are there sports activities that figure into your experience? How is your body socioculturally read in relation to your skill in the particular sport? Gender, size, race?

- ☑ Was there physical trauma involved in your experience? Physical abuse? Though you may or may not want to include the physical details, critically reflect upon how/why these details affected your perceptions/views/behaviors.

Ethics

What are the ethical implications of representing others in autoethnography? This element is arguably the most significant in performative autoethnography as it is the foundation of the performative-I disposition, the textualizing body, the aesthetic/epistemic imperative, and agency and representation. The performative-I disposition is based upon the willingness to examine one's own values, beliefs and biases. Some of the most effective autoethnographies take the reader/audience through the autoethnographer's process of opening up and critically reflecting upon his or her value-laden perspectives, biases, and taken for granted assumptions.

In his popular article, "Performing as a Moral Act: Ethical Dimensions of the Ethnography of Performance" (1982), Dwight

Conquergood offers a mapping of ethical pitfalls which may occur in the representation of, or critical reflection upon, others within the context. These ethical pitfalls describe problematic and unethical stances toward representing the other in ethnographic fieldwork and as such, are especially applicable to autoethnography as the roots of autoethnography are embedded in critical ethnographic fieldwork.

Conquergood's metaphoric conceptualizations of ethically problematic stances provide a vocabulary with which to analyze and articulate ethically problematic approaches—or dispositions—that the researcher might enact in the autoethnographic research and writing process. Conquergood's approaches include, *The Custodian's Rip-off, The Enthusiast's Infatuation, The Curator's Exhibitionism, and The Skeptic's Cop-out.* Working off these conceptualizations I have added *The Hero, The Blamer,* and *The Victim* as particular to performative autoethnography.

I encourage the reader to engage these approaches with a pedagogical rather than pejorative mindset. Critical reflection itself is often about reexamining motives and methods of our own misdeeds or mistakes. *Shame and blame can establish an irreconcilable block in such critical self-reflection, making it nearly impossible to learn and grow from our mistakes and debilitating assumptions.* So, rather than approaching these concepts by seeking to prove how you have never or would never enact these ethical pitfalls, please critically reflect upon the how/why/where in which you—as all of us do based on our own baises and prejudices—enact these unethical methods of representation. Remember that performative autoethnography seeks to reveal the processes of interrupting our own and others' perpetuation of oppression so that it may be generative and pedagogical.

The Custodian's Rip-off is characterized by selfishness and ambition. Here the researcher focuses upon any part of an experience that will be *shocking or dramatic* to the audience. Conquergood states that the researcher has an "overriding motive of 'finding good performance material'" (6) rather than seeking to understand the differences and difficulties of cultural interaction. Others are represented by the researcher in exaggerated ways that serve the drama of the autoethnography, often framing the researcher as hero or victim.

Researchers in this stance are more concerned with shocking the audience, or getting published, rather than representing the conflicts and collisions of cultural differences with dignity and balance. A researcher may, for instance, use the pain and tragedy of others or other historic cultural trauma, like the Holocaust for example, to represent his experience as more "meaningful" or dramatic. The researcher may engage in *shocking self-disclosure* by purposefully foregrounding the traumatic details and events of a difficult experience without connecting this trauma to rigorous critical reflection. "Self-reflexive does *not* mean self-indulgent" (148), writes Goodall (2008).

Thick description of events must always be in the service of generating knowledge through critical reflection; certainly transformative life events can be shocking in their degree of trauma, but *the autoethnographer thickly describes trauma for the purpose of critically reflecting upon the ways in which traumatic events are epistemologically connected to larger social issues.* In the unethical stance of The Custodian's Rip-off, little regard is shown for deep critical reflection upon self, other, context, or of the autoethnographic process.

The Blamer: The process of critical reflection is not possible within self blame. Though blaming oneself may be the *initial* response in reflecting upon an experience, blame prevents the process of examining and *taking responsibility for the representation* of our own experiences and for becoming a social theorist (Butler 2005). In "From Goldilocks to Dreadlocks" I examine my own internalized racism and try to track its origins through my upbringing. Blaming and shaming will not allow me to critically reflect upon my own behaviors. *Blaming self* and stopping there lets one off the critical hook; it stops the pedagogical process of learning from our connections to others in larger social systems and from our involvement in perpetuating or being subject to oppressive systems.

Blaming other and stopping there also lets one off the critical hook. Examining sociocultural norms and expectations that may have been operating in the decisions made by others can open another level of critique. For example, in "Call It Swing," I critically reflect upon the ways in which my dad challenged and perpetuated racism; simply blaming him for racist decisions blocks the pedagogical potential of autoethnography. After critiquing a particular situation, I write:

> In reality of course, I have no idea what was going through his mind in those next mornings when he walked out the front door, onto the bus, and then up to the bandstand for the next gig. But I do know that critically reflecting upon the possibilities of who he may have been with others in those contexts engenders knowledge that interrupts the silence or hegemonic narratives of racial privilege. (275)

Performative autoethnography must be about personal/political accountability and ethical agency, not blame.

The Hero: Ethical performative autoethnography is not a hero's tale either. Autoethnography can sometimes become a tale of heroics rather than a critical reflection upon the complexities of social inequities. One is not heroic, for example, for taking the necessary responsibility for understanding the effects of privilege. Analyzing one's own oppressive acts takes courage, but/and must be written with the *humility* that keeps cultural hubris always in check. *Sociocultural accountability is human, not heroic.*

The Victim: On the other hand, critically reflecting upon the personal as political can engender a framing of self as victim without offering a deeper critical analysis. This can be a difficult ethical consideration since much of autoethnography's potential as a method of change focuses upon the ways in which inequity and injustice affect our everyday lives. *But as a method of scholarly inquiry,* performative autoethnography must move the analysis deeper into critically examining the sociocultural systems sustaining the injustice. Amanda's autoethnography serves as an example of the researcher taking us through the details of her assault and then critiquing her high school classmate's reactions as illustrative of dominant cultural narratives that try to minimize the severity of assault by shaming the survivor. Performative autoethnography can be empowering, but not at the expense of rigorous critical reflection and ethical representation.

Enthusiast's Infatuation: This stance is characterized by a facile and unreflective identification with the other or cultural context. All differences between self and other are denied or ignored with a glib and over-romaticized "We're all just the same on the inside!" kind of approach to cultural differences. Here the researcher may behave in a self-righteous manner claiming that he or she is "colorblind" and does not "see" differences between people, as if seeing difference is crass, ignorant, or insulting. *It is only those with racial privilege who have the hubris to claim to be "colorblind," or blind to gender, class, religion or other cultural differences.* Those without privilege are *fully* aware of differences as they are reminded of them daily by not being listened to or taken seriously in a meeting, or being followed in a store by "security," or being inherently suspected of terrorist activities (I am not talking about white males in this last example, though it was a white male who enacted the first contemporary terrorist bombing in the U. S.—Oklahoma City).

In the stance of Enthusiast's Infatuation, the other can do no wrong and is represented only in the most glowing terms creating a patronizing one-dimensional non-critical portrayal of otherness. The other is described as being without flaw in an almost "protective" manner. Within a protective frame, the other is often represented as perpetual victim, thus patronizing and depoliticizing the other.

Curator's Exhibitionism: "Whereas the enthusiast assumed too easy identification with the other," writes Conquergood, "the curator is committed to the Difference of the other" (7). Within this stance, others are represented as exotic, primitive, culturally antique. Here Native Americans are perceived as wearing feathered headdresses, African Americas are always athletic, and women are always nurturing. Within this stance, the other is often viewed as a "noble savage." Ojibwe Indians, for example, were exalted as "noble" warriors and then forced to attend Christian schools where they were required to dress like white people and punished for using their language due to their perceived "savagery." Today, a researcher might seek to exult American nationalism by using Native Americans as a "pure" and "authentic" American image, leaving out, of course, the history of the Trail of Tears massacre or contemporary reservation politics. Concomitantly, others are put on a pedestal, revered, displayed, appreciated as a cultural artifact or object, as culturally "authentic." As in the other problematic stances, no critical reflection occurs about self-other interaction, sociocultural context, or social construction of body.

Research, research, research. Do not expect others to "educate" you about a particular history, culture, or political situation. Preparation is one of the highest forms of respect toward others in the research context. For example, in "Call It Swing," I critically reflect upon the ways in which race impacted my dad's everyday life during his years as a jazz drummer. Though I grew up with my dad, I needed to spend months researching jazz and its connection to race before I could engage in substantive critical analysis about the sociocultural context within which my dad played.

With these conceptualizations and considerations in mind, what ethical pitfalls may occur in your representation of, or critical self-reflection upon, self within the context? Other? (See the writing exercises at the end of the chapter for further exploration.)

These are the elements of composing performative autoethnography; they comprise the content of the writing. Whenever you find yourself stuck or in writer's block, go back to the questions prompting the critical reflection of each element. As mentioned earlier, each element figures into the construction of the text, but the degree to which each one functions is dependent on the autoethnographer's experience and what he wants to focus on. The elements constitute the function of words/language in the construction of the textualizing body.

The elements of composing autoethnography address the content of your writing. Now we will focus on the *form* of performative autoethnographic writing.

Form: How Should It Look on the Page?

The text you write can take ANY form, i.e. poetic, essay, etc. Think of how form might function with the descriptors of performative writing: embodied, coperformed, evocative, and consequential. The performative autoethnographic text should reflect how the words/language perform in/on the body. Think of how Gingrich-Philbrook lives "body-language-body-language" (1999) and how this is illustrated in his work "Bite Your Tongue." Feel the vulnerability of Pineau's autoethnographic body-language in "Nursing Mother" (2000):

> And so they begin. Robin, Mary, Ellen, Sue, Bob, Nancy, Francis, Tom, Dick, and Harry put their hands on your body. Just relax. They put your feet in the stirrups, just relax, push open your knees, just relax, snap on their gloves, just relax...and they *peer*. (7)

Through her thick description we *feel* the eyes, the hands, surely, the *words* on her body. The aesthetic form of the sentences, the choice of words has as much to do with the politics of the medical world as it does with the personal of Elyse's experience. We see the importance of aesthetic form in the episteme of her work that allows us to feel the politics of the personal.

Remember "Skins: A Daughter's (Re)Construction of Cancer" at the beginning of chapter 1:

> I remember waking up in the middle of the night to a
>
> BANG BANG BANG.
>
> It was faint but *very* direct.
>
> My father and I were light sleepers during this time
>
> because my mother had to sleep downstairs in a hospital bed.

She was too weak to climb the stairs.

BANG BANG BANG.

I went to the top of the stairs and looked down into the darkness. Mom was having trouble sleeping and wanted all the lights off.
I went down the stairs and flipped the hall light on and

BANG BANG BANG... (2003, 215).

Notice the shortened length of the lines and the capitalization of words. I wanted the reader or audience to see and feel on the page how I felt as I looked down into the darkness hearing that sound, the sound we then find out is my mother alone and in pain in the dark. We want the body to "perform" on the page. Remember performative autoethnography engages the textualizing body where writing and the movement of the body are dependent upon one another.

Fragments

In composing autoethnography it is difficult to know how, where, or with what to begin. As in the discussion in chapter 1 about the fragmented subjectivity and form of autoethnography, begin thinking and writing in *fragments of experience*. Fragments might take the form of a word or list of words, an image, a metaphor, a sentence, or any "idea as they come alive within and through people(s), communities, events, texts…" (Grande 2008, 233). Begin generating fragments by *brainstorming* ANY fragment or piece or part of an experience. This would include any interaction, conversation, places/spaces/towns/cities lived in, a particular house/room/building/church/bedroom/bar, particular people/family/friends, a particular gathering of people/family/friends, a line or paragraph addressing elements of composing, etc.

When in the process of generating fragments, *do not worry how or why a fragment might work or how it would be put together in a story.*

Some will be used and some will be put aside for another project, but you cannot make those decisions at this point since you don't know what the focus of the script will be. The process of writing is the process of dis/un/recovering your thoughts and ideas about your topic. Though a fragment itself may seem insignificant, it may certainly initiate or be a bridge to other key pieces. As you begin this process, your mind/body will start to call up experiences that you may not have thought of for many years. Through your writing move yourself into the physical, environmental, and emotional recollection of the experience fragment.

A fragment might also consist of a piece of fiction or non-fiction literature, news article, or YouTube video that is significant to the experience in some way. In his autoethnography dealing with the complexities of father-son relationships, a student played clips from movies where a father and son were "having a catch" with a baseball or football. When putting his autoethnography together, the student didn't know how or if he was going to use the clips, only that they were each a fragment that connected to his experience in some way.

The elements of composing performative autoethnography will generate fragments. Look through the questions posed in the five elements (sociocultural context, critical self-reflection, self-other interaction, the body, ethics) and answer each one. Do not judge the reason for, or the quality of, the writing at this point. Generating fragments is the goal.

A fragment may also be thought of as a scene within a particular experience. Consider the example on page 122 in "From Goldilocks to Dreadlocks" (2001b). This passage began as a separate fragment in the form of a scene. In thinking about how race has intersected my life, this scene was very significant in its illustration of white privilege. At the time I wrote this fragment I didn't know how or where it would fit in the autoethnography, I just knew it was significant. Writing this fragment generated other memories and critical reflection. But you must write to figure this out. The process of writing is the process of discovery.

Carry a notebook devoted only to the autoethnography, prefer-
ably one that feels good in your hands, one that opens to you easily
both physically and emotionally. Have the notebook handy as often
as possible because once begun, critical reflection is not easily turned
off. Meanings about experiences, recollections of events will begin
coming, unbidden, into the tasks of daily life. Autoethnography is
transformative, and as such opens our thought processes up in unpre-
dictable ways. You may be having coffee, doing dishes, falling off to
sleep when a critical fragment of experience reveals itself.

Mindmap

At this point there will most likely be a cascade of fragments, an
overwhelming number of pieces of the story. Recalling or critically
reflecting upon events, people, ideas will cause a continual multitude
of connections to come tumbling out. Create mindmaps to begin
some organized connection to the fragments. Mindmaps can also be
used as a brainstorming device.

To create a mindmap, draw a small circle in the middle of notebook paper; write a word in the circle that you think may be a focus
or major fragment of the experience. Then literally draw lines outward from the middle circle. At the ends of these lines, draw a circle
containing a word that connects with the one in the middle. Draw
connections from these circles, etc. Again, *do not question why* you
are making these connections at this point. Just let your critical
imagination (Denzin 2006) do its work.

Make as many mindmaps as you like. This is the beginning of
organizing the autoethnography into clusters.

Clusters

After a number of fragments have been generated, begin thinking
about how the disparate fragments might be connected. Mindmaps
are an effective way to begin to see connection between fragments.
As you continue making mindmaps, clusters will begin to emerge.
These clusters may be loosely thought of as "main points" in the

autoethnography. In "Call It Swing," all I knew when I began generating fragments and making clusters was that I wanted to explore how my dad negotiated race as a musician in jazz. Themes or main points slowly began to emerge that included the function of jazz swing as a subversive methodology in analyzing race, and the employment of swing as a conceptualizing tool for autoethnography. As these main points or themes emerge begin further development of the fragments.

Thick Description

To begin fleshing out the fragments, develop what Clifford Geertz called a "thick description" of the experience. Describe the events in detail, deciding what detail an audience will need to hear, see, feel, etc. to dialogically engage performance. Try thinking in terms of describing who, what, when, where, etc.

Develop a "thick description" of your emotional experience as well, or your "emotional intelligence" about the experience. Describe your thoughts, feelings, attitudes, emotions during the event(s) and during the process of critical reflection.

As you continue to write, thick descriptions of events, emotion, and critique will merge into one another. Consider thick description in this passage from "Tattoo Stories" about my grandmother. I write:

We would drive quickly in the dark, get to my aunt's house,
and there Gram would be,
lying on the couch
stiff,
still,
paralyzed,
her jaw locked,
her eyes half way open.
Sometimes Gram would   moan
through her clenched teeth

and we would all rush over

leaning close

trying to hear,

all of us leaning over her,

my Mom,   my three aunts,   and me,

all of us

leaning over watching bits

and pieces of ourselves   breaking

in Gram's

distorted face. (92)

Notice the thick description of my gram's body. This passage was a result of considering the composition element of body in terms of the possible genetic inheritance of mental illness in my family.

Notice also in the passage how form is affected by the rhythm of speech and emotion, the cadence of the body's experience; the writing is seeking to perform the body.

Research

Research is used to support and expand upon the critical reflection, analysis, and representations explicated in your autoethnography. *Think of research as a voice in the conversation of your work.* As mentioned in the composition element of ethics, research the sociocultural issues and structures at play in your experience. For example, if a student is critically reflecting upon how manhood is played out in the military, the student might research studies on masculinity in communication and performance studies, gender studies, or sociology. How does the research dialogue with different fragments of your autoethnography?

Think of *research as being in concert or conversation with your critical imagination.* Rather than thinking of research as only supporting a scholarly point, think of it as a conversation you are having with the ideas or author. This is part of the aesthetic responsibility in epistemology, in creating knowledge. For example, in "Goldilocks to Dreadlocks":

I am in the bathroom of a disco, circa 1980.

I am White, 19, 110 pounds, blonde,

and command the gaze of most men

in this mostly Black disco.

Four Black women
follow me into the bathroom.
Standing in front of the mirror,
I whip out my brush.
"They" are firmly planted
too close,
behind me.

We use the mirror as our looking glass.
We use the mirror
to reify Black, White, Pretty, Sexy.
Kate Davy says that "white womanhood
is a racialization process
played out on many fronts,"
not the least of which positions
the black woman as sexual monster
and the white woman as sexually
innocent, pure, and gentile,
authorized by the dictates
of white womanhood. (210–211)

We look into this glass
for refraction, not reflection.
We fracture ourselves
busting each other's chops
into the one dimensional
looking glass. (2001b, 57–58)

In this passage, the research is in conversation with the critique. The aesthetic form of the passage suggests that this research and the autoethnographer are speaking with and of one another.

Research can also be used in dissonance with your story. Maybe your experience is in contrast with popular or academic research. Many indigenous scholars such as Sandy Grande and Linda Tuhiwai Smith intentionally refute scholarship done about indigenous peoples by non-indigenous researchers to reveal colonizing and imperialist methods and findings. Also note how the form in which the research is presented functions on the page.

> How is this passage an example of the aesthetic/epistemic imperative discussed earlier?

Remember, autoethnography is not just the articulation of a personal story; the autoethnographer is articulating critical cultural knowledge that is intended to be epistemologically generative for an audience, to be "equipment for living" (Burke 1989) in our everyday lives. *The autoethnographer is generating scholarship.* Research should illustrate/support the sociocultural issues in the performance, i.e. if your performance deals with divorce, what are the statistics of divorce, what do interpersonal communication scholars or psychology studies say about your experience as, for example, a child or parent of divorce? How does your experience agree or disagree with this research?

Let the composition elements guide your research. Engage research from course readings where you might be commenting on the process of how you are using autoethnography and performance to explore the issue. In this way the performative autoethnography is commenting on process while producing product.

Metaphor

Use metaphor in your writing to expand and deepen meaning of the experiences. Theorists argue that we understand our world through metaphor, i.e. the use of sports metaphors and war metaphors (Lakoff and Johnson 1980). Objects can often symbolize complex issues and experiences causing us to make deeper associations and connections. Metaphors can be objects, places, ideas. Make a list of objects and places that are in some way connected with any part of your experience. Consider what each one might symbolize in the construction of your experience. For example, consider the way in which skin is used as a metaphor in "Skins: A Daughter's (Re)Construction of Cancer" to expand and give dimension to issues of gender identification and class.

Metaphors can be an organizing construct. In "From Goldilocks to Dreadlocks" hair is a metaphor symbolizing the larger sociopolitical ramifications of beauty and race; it is then used to organize the clusters creating the text. Remember that metaphors are culturally constructed. A metaphor that works in one cultural context or language system may not convey the same meaning in another.

Time and Space

Critically reflecting upon a transformative event may require you to go back and forth through time and space. Though it is a story, performative autoethnography is seldom chronological due to its fragmentation; this allows many more possibilities in terms of form. Maybe the autoethnography begins with a scene from childhood, then jumps to a narrative revealing your thought processes as a child compared with how you make sense of the experience now.

The autoethnography may present a particular self-other interaction, a conversation that happened in the past, followed immediately by the autoethnographer stepping out of the scene to reveal what she is thinking during the conversation. Look back at "Tattoo Stories" and think about how many times and places are presented. How do these differing times and places assist in the effectiveness of the autoethnography? How do they connect the personal and political allowing critical reflection upon a larger issue or idea? Consider a passage from "Call It Swing":

> Who is to say then, what went through my dad's mind in those times, and surely they were many, when systems of power and privilege would collide at two a.m. at a motel on a dark road in a small town in 1940s southern America? In this coperformative moment, how are the stakes different for each of these musicians seeking to maintain equilibrium with style? What is happening in that moment of decision making when a white person is betwixt and between interruption or perpetuation, between embracing or challenging h/h own privilege?
>
> For example, what was he expected to do by the white people who owned the motel? Was my dad at risk if he choose not to walk through the front door? Further, how might he have put his band mates at risk through his defiance? How often have white people tried to "teach each other a lesson" at the expense of people of color creating a difficult situation, or worse, placing them in jeopardy with a retaliatory racist (Spry 2008)? Jimmie Lunceford's death for example is attributed to poisoning by a racist restaurant owner who loathed feeding the Lunceford band (Daniels). Surely my father's success as a respected musician, as *a musician who could swing,*
>
> *(begin slow finger snap)*
>
> depended upon deft negotiations of these liminal moments.
>
> *(Begin to sing the text intermittently)* Did he and the band "play" these racists coperformatively,

improvising and listening deeply for the right note, the right rhythm, the right tim(ing)e to drop into the bridge for a solo just in time *(sing) Just in time, I found you just in time, just in time...* for this particular audience? *(End singing)* Jazz "dwells not just in one solo at a time," notes Vijay Iyer, "but in an entire lifetime of improvisations" (395). Surely improvisation is a main component in the art of racial code switching. Being "the only white boy," my dad must have spent years observing the subversive jazz swing of code switching from people whose lives depended on it. He must have known the consequences of the wrong note at the wrong time. They knew the musical score for this middle-of-the-night middle-of-the-South performance, and must have depended upon their abilities to body forth together, to collaborate, to coperform, to swing. (2010, 275)

I go back and forth through time from talking about my dad in the present day, coupled with a scene at a motel in the South, circa 1940, where, as a white man, he was the only man in the band allowed through the front door. I then move to a fragment discussing how he must have learned the art of racial code switching by watching his band members switch their communication styles when talking to racist white people in ways that would ensure their safety in the 1940s South. Messing with time and space allows the autoethnographer to place particular scenes, ideas, critiques next to each other that deepen the meaning of the text.

Additional Persona

A persona is any other person that might exist in your autoethnography. Your autoethnography might include a persona other than you, someone significant to your understanding and meaning making of the experience. This writing most likely emerges from the self-other interaction composition element. Who is it and why is he/she important? For example, Pineau might include a narrative of, or conversation with, her mother, or her doctor.

The persona can be fictional. You may want to create a persona who embodies the voice(s) of dominant sociocultural expectations. For example, in Amanda's autoethnography she might create a persona who embodies dominant cultural narratives that encourage women to stay silent about assault, "What were you wearing? Had you been drinking? Did you fight back?" A scene or dialogue might be created between the autoethnographer and the fictional persona that illustrates a particular aspect of critical analysis. A persona can be woven throughout the autoethnography. We might revisit persona for various reasons, perhaps to show the progression, or regression, of a relationship.

Now. Start Writing. Now.

We can talk and read and think all day about writing. But now it's time to walk through the threshold. The best way to start writing is to start writing. Begin fleshing out the fragments in your mindmaps. Rather than having a preconceived goal or ending or meaning, let the fragments take you to where they want to go. The fleshing out of one fragment will affect the form and content of others. Always consult the elements of composing performative autoethnography if you are stuck or need focus.

Resist shortcuts. Sometimes it is tempting to tell a story and then quickly tack a connection to larger social issues on the end. This practice does not constitute performative autoethnography. Critical reflection is part and parcel of thick description, metaphor, scenes, persona, fragments, etc.

Structuring Performative Autoethnography: From Fragments to Collage.

With the writing underway, begin considering how the text might be structured.

The process of critical reflection is seldom linear. Speaking from my own experience, fragments, pieces of self, spirit, whathaveyou, do not eventually coalesce into a coherent subject. Rather, they recognize one another in breakage, remaking alternate ways of being. Yes, messy, argumentative, compassionate, and comforting.

Since performative autoethnography is located in the intersections of lived experience and larger social issues, constructing meaning from these intersections often happens as if constructing a critical collage. The autoethnography may take us back and forth through time and space and thought for the purpose of showing the critical connections made through the particular construction of the collage.

For example, in writing "Paper and Skin" about the grief process, I had the sensation that my body began falling apart in pieces around me, and it was in this sense of wreckage that I began to see inconsistency and fragment as the form and function of my grief and its autoethnographic representation. Through writing, I began to feel a deep somatic connection to that fractured self and space, a space I would later describe as a performative-I disposition. "It is," as Pollock says, "a space of absence made present in desire and imagination, through which readers may pass like shadows or fiends." (1998, 86). I let myself remember that we live experience directly and study it performatively. I embraced my body, as Madison suggests, "as the feeling/sensing home of our being—the vulnerability of how our body must move through the space and time of another—transporting our very being and breath—," the being and breath of our son, "for the purpose of knowledge" (2009, 191).

As the performative autoethnographer articulates experience through language, the language turns back upon itself changing, redefining, breaking and remaking one's understanding of the negotiation between self, other, and context within the transformative experience. Body and word, experience and craft are simultaneously reformulating meaning, revealing possibilities for transgressive voices and multiple stories in the world. It is a living and "wording" of the textualizing body. Rather than a space of endings or answers the aesthetic/epistemic praxis offers a continuation of meaning and transformation.

Performative autoethnography asks a lot of a person. It asks you to lay yourself open to the scrutiny of your own critique. The anecdote, "We are our own worst critic," applies only when shame and blame are involved. Otherwise, the gentle, rigorous, scholarly, personal, communal, intuitive critical reflection upon our human blunders and successes can offer local knowledge with global consequences. We are responsible for telling stories.

Warm-ups for Writing Performative Autoethnography

Though the elements for composing performative autoethnography are themselves designed to prompt writing, these warm-ups approach certain elements from another angle and might assist in beginning and continuing the writing process. Come back to the warm-ups—as well as the composition elements—when you feel stuck in your writing or do not know how to begin a particular fragment or section.

1. Write a short paragraph for each of the questions in the *elements for composing* performative autoethnography. Write a paragraph even if you don't think it applies to your experience.

2. *Create a mindmap:* Write a paragraph for each circle connected to the center circle.

3. *Identifying metaphors:* Brainstorm a list of objects that are related to your experience in some way; make a list all the way down the page.

   a. Make a mindmap for four or five of the metaphors concerning what they might symbolize.

   b. Choose four or five of the metaphors and write a paragraph about what each one symbolizes in the larger scheme of your experience.

4. *Sociocultural expectations:* Brainstorm a list of sociocultural expectations that you feel apply to you in your everyday life. In other words, what are the performativities expected of you as white, black, disabled, female, gay, or Somali living in the U.S., etc.

   a. Turn these expectations/performativities into statements that you may have already heard.

   b. Write a paragraph for each statement critically reflecting upon how the statement affects your experience.

5. *Body:* Do the same exercise as number 4 for your body.

6. *Self-other interaction:* Brainstorm a list of people related to your experience in any way, past or present, living or not.

   a. If there was an interaction with the other:

      i. Write a paragraph describing the interaction, or write out the dialogue as you remember it.

      ii. Then write a paragraph describing what you were thinking at the time during the interaction.

      iii. Write a paragraph describing what you think of the interaction now. How does this differ from (ii)?

      iv. Write a paragraph describing how you *wish or thought* the interaction was going to occur.

   b. Write a paragraph concerning what you think the other may have been thinking. In "Call It Swing," I infer what my dad may have been thinking during the incident at a motel when he was allowed in the front door and his African-American bandmates were asked to enter through the back door.

7. *Ethics:* Write a paragraph describing yourself as inhabiting each of the ethical pitfalls. Though some of the pitfalls may not seem to apply to you or your experience, this exercise will

crack open critical insight into your own values, beliefs, attitudes, and behaviors.

8. *Mess with time*: Describe an event in your experience from the point of view of yourself as a child or as yourself much older.

   a. Be specific in terms of age range. Two-to-four years old is a different narrative than 6–8 or 10–12.

   b. Remember to use language as you would have as a child.

   c. AS ALWAYS remember not to create a stereotype of "child" or "old person"; this, as in all autoethnographic writing, is a specific person who happens to be a child or elderly rather than a stereotyped performativity of such.

Chapter
Four

Stage
Performing the
Autoethnographic Body

*Experiencing language as a transformative force was not an
awareness that I arrived at through writing. I discovered it
through performance.*

bell hooks, *Remembered Rapture: The Writer at Work,* 35

Why Perform Autoethnography?

Critical theorist bell hooks answers the above question. Performance is the experiencing of language. And for the performative autoethnographer, performance is discovering the transformative force of experiencing the language of her body, experiencing the language she chose to ethically represent her body's communions and collisions with others in culture. How are we transformed through performing/embodying the words we have written? How are the words transformed through performance? These fundamental questions turn us back upon the overall purpose of this book: to present an autoethnographic method for an *engaged, critical, and embodied pedagogy, in other words, learning from and in the performance of autoethnography.*

From "Paper and Skin: Bodies of Loss and Life"

I lay on a massage table. Deb, my dear friend and Rieki Master, is doing energy work on me. As I lay on the table, gently, gingerly, my arms snap off my body like sandstone or peanut brittle. It is a clean break. And it is in this dismemberment that I begin to feel relief from the weight of empty arms.

In delivering this story, a scream inhabits my words. During delivery I was engulfed from behind by waves of wails, horrendous echoes from a million years of a billion women who have delivered this story. The whispers of their body's knowledge was a shock wave pushing me forward and causing my body to produce a sssssooooooouuuuunnnnndddddd that I could not recognize as my own. After 5 months of pregnancy, I heard my voice in concert with an ancient wail of women.

It is the incoherency of it all. Bombs have gone off in my life, and rather than running around trying to put bodies of words back together, as I have done in the past, I find that I can only watch and witness as the dismemberings bleed a syntax of fractioned sentence structures.

The words are unmeshed in the blood and bones of the mother and child. Arms ache and disarm themselves with the visceral absence of the other. Writing doesn't help me put my arms back on, but it does help me to remember that I had arms, and then, to show me that the arms are still usable in a way I can't yet understand.

In performing "Paper and Skin," I embodied words that allowed me to make sense of grief and loss and absence, to *feel and experience* myself as a grieving mother in a nation grieving 9/11. Performing crafted critical stories of loss put me back into a body that I had abandoned, brought a presence to absence, allowing me to again embrace my body "as the feeling/sensing home of our being—the vulnerability of how our body must move through the space and time of another" (Madison 2009, 191).

In performing autoethnography, the researcher begins the process of moving the body from the page to the stage. He begins trying on the self negotiated through the performative-I disposition of writing. In trying on this body of words, this linguistic body, there will necessarily be parts that fit like a glove, parts that tear at the seams, parts that simply require alteration for the hearts and hands that made them. The process of performing autoethnography then, is a continuation of the writing process, a synergistic transference from the performance-I *disposition* to the performative-I *persona*. Embodying performative autoethnography is the process of embodying the performative-I persona in performance. The performative-I persona is the person, the subject, the "you," created in the autoethnographic text.

In the next two chapters, we will work through a clear methodological process of performance, a process of bringing the body from the page to the stage called the *Elements of an Embodied Performance*. Like composing performative autoethnography, *performing* performative autoethnography is a method of inquiry and analysis that engages the body as the methodological nexus upon which the text turns, move, lives. It is the manifestation of the textualizing body where no epistemological hierarchy exists between researching/body, writing/paper, and performing/stage; all are equally present and accountable in the meaning-making process. This chapter will provide the necessary theoretical groundwork for performing autoethnography; in chapter 5 then, we will engage the elements of an embodied performance.

As recognized in the introductory chapter, to move into a substantive engagement of performance, one must have a firm grounding in the theoretical and methodological work in performance. Because embodiment is as essential in performance as it is in the composition process, we will discuss the weight and responsibility of proper preparation when embodying the moral discourse of autoethnography; the concept *practiced vulnerability* will be offered as a threshold into the process of embodiment. This chapter will then undertake the question of who and what we are performing in performative autoethnography by conceptualizing self as a performative-I persona. Though we will make a distinction between *performer* and *persona,* both are bound in a continual process of becoming.

Conceptualizing Performance

Moving from our discussion in chapter 1, in *Body,Paper,Stage* performance is conceptualized as constitutive of sociocultural realities (realities are created by how we perform in society), as epistemic (performance creates knowledge), and as a method of critique. Performance fulfills these functions through embodiment of language. As an embodied method of study and inquiry, performance explicates how and why we make the choices we do in the socially constructed, creative, contingent, and collaborative dimensions of selves and others communicating in culture. Creativity, culture, and critique characterize our relationship to performance. In "Performance Studies: Interventions and Radical Research," one of his many ground-breaking essays, Dwight Conquergood offers a multiplicity of interconnected summations about performance that undergird this book. We view performance as:

> **Analysis:** the interpretation of art and culture; critical reflection; thinking about, through and with performance; performance as a lens that illuminates the constructed creative, contingent, collaborative dimensions of human communication; knowledge that comes from contemplation and comparison; concentrated attention and contextualization as a way of knowing.

> **Accomplishment:** the making of art and remaking of culture; creativity; embodiment; artistic process and form; knowledge that comes from doing, performativity; participatory understanding; performing as a way of knowing.

> **Articulation:** activism, outreach, connection to community; applications and interventions; action research; projects that

reach outside the academy and are rooted in an ethic of reciprocity and exchange; knowledge that is tested by practice within a community; social commitment, collaboration, and contribution/intervention as a way of knowing; praxis. (319)

We embrace performance as a method of "intellectual rebellion," (Thomas 1993), as a method of localized global critique, as "a radical critical pedagogy of hope" (Denzin 2006, 330). Performative autoethnography seeks to identify and call into question performances of class, race, and gender marked as normative which restrict and belay alternative ways of being. In *Critical Ethnography: Method, Ethics, and Performance*, D. Soyini Madison employs a method and theory nexus of performance ethnography integral to our view of performance in autoethnography:

> Think of a project in your community that might benefit through writing and performing autoethnography. Write a paragraph describing one of the benefits.

to articulate and identify hidden forces and ambiguities that operate beneath appearances; to guide judgments and evaluations emanating from our discontent; to demystify the ubiquity and magnitude of power; to provide insight and inspire acts of justice; and to name and analyze what is intuitively felt. (2005, 13)

The danger of a single story of culture, a single dominant performance of power, is articulated, challenged, and deposed by performative autoethnography by its creation of socioculturally transgressive stories of reality.

We live experience directly, but study it performatively (Spry 2010). Lived experience is analyzed through theories of embodiment and enfleshed methodologies, because our bodies are always and already painfully and ecstatically present as we try to understand and articulate "the conditions of our emergence" with others in contexts

(Butler 2005). Embedded in the performative turn toward ethnography and the ethnographic turn toward performance (Spry 2006), the development of performative autoethnography as method, as process and product, our conceptualizations about what it *is* and what it *does* have become, for me at least, deeply generative in understanding the personal politics of pain, loss, and hope as we live with others in an often unjustifiable and uneven local/global system of power. It is, as Dwight Conquergood says, a "performance-sensitive way of knowing" (1998, 26) that empowers Amanda to dismantle experiences of misogyny, entitles Anthony to articulate alternative stories of Black masculinity, and motivates Trenton to speak queer critique from the pews of a church.

As explicated in the introduction, the methodological processes of analysis, composition, and performance are deemed interdependent through the concept of a textualizing body where no epistemological hierarchy exists between page, stage, word, or body; the body/self, the autoethnographic text, and the performance of the text contribute equally to the meaning making process. In performative autoethnography, performance does not operate as an interesting feature or entertaining option that one might choose after "finishing" the autoethnography. Here, performance does not "illuminate" the text, rather it assists in the creation of the text; it is in itself performative.

The composition and performance process continually forms and reforms the performative body, the body of the text, the text of the body. Performance is a heuristic tool, not an added scholarly bonus. The textualizing body is always on the move, continually un/re/made through analysis, writing, and performance.

The Weight of Performative Embodiment: Putting Flesh on the Bones of Discourse

As bell hooks (1999) asserts, she discovered the "transformative force" of language through performing language. Having articulated critique through the elements for composing performative autoethnography, we now prepare to move the body from page to stage, and self into the process of embodying a performative-I persona. In doing so, there is much to consider about the somatic engagement of performance.

Think about an excerpt from "Yet To Name," a work by a Meggie Mapes, a former student in performative autoethnography:

> *I remember long pink fingernails. The fingernails of a woman's name that doesn't come to mind, sitting behind a desk, making sure I had made a sound and "informed" decision.*
>
> *I remember the room to wait. Five of us sat in a small room wearing a hospital style gown and booties. A room where we were given valium at the same time. There were no words; no visual connection that we were women experiencing a life changing event at the same time. We were quiet, we were silent, we were shameful.*
>
> *I remember being in a box. But unlike the sturdy walls of a box, I had no support.*
>
> *I remember looking at the ultrasound. I was asked to look, forced.*
>
> *"What is that? What could it be?"*
>
> *Angela Laflen writes how we immediately picture the silhouette of a fetus. There's no possible way a silhouette existed only seven weeks in but that woman stood over me and asked me to look, to create a silhouette for me.*
>
> *I remember being the last of five to go in. I don't know how much time had passed but the valium had put me to sleep and probably worn off because the whole thing hurt like hell. Yes, it was painful. Before, during, and after.*
>
> *I remember the mechanics. The mechanical treatment of me, my body, my mind. I remember being mechanical. Processing how a good feminist is supposed to act when terminating a pregnancy. I joked in the waiting room, spoke with confidence to the nurses, I was confident, right?*
>
> *I remember being judged.*
>
> *I remember feeling guilty that I didn't feel anything inside me. What kind of a woman was I? I felt guilty for not having morning sickness, for not being sick even though I felt sick. Wasn't that what a real feminist felt like?*

I remember being ashamed. Not outright. Every relationship I began after terminating began with a confession. Within days there was a confession.

"I had an abortion."

Why? I was ashamed. If someone thinks you've committed murder, it's a deal breaker.

I remember feeling selfish.

I was one of those feminists. The kind that say "I support the decision to choose but I would never make that choice." I was 20, single, halfway through college, living on loans and scholarship money. What kind of choice is that?

I am now one of those feminists. The kind that remember what I've done and the experiences I've had. The kind that believe in the choice but believe in the knowledge to make that choice. This is a confession. A confession to force a dialogue, a new dialogue on the reality surrounding women. As Leslie Cannold in her book The Abortion Myth *says, "women don't own their bodies, they are their bodies" (22). A doctor whose name I don't know, a doctor who didn't know my name, a doctor who became faceless behind his mask, laid me on a table and manipulated my body. I wasn't ignorant to what was happening between my legs and under the thin blue cloth. That cloth couldn't cover what was happening to my body, mine. Was it my choice? Yes. Because of that choice, I am one of those feminists. I'll sacrifice the privacy of my body once again on the pages of this paper in hopes that sacrifice isn't in vain. Women have abortions. Women **feel** about their abortions. I am a woman. I had an abortion.*

Consider how Ms. Mapes's work illustrates Conquergood's summations of performance as analysis, accomplishment, and articulation. Think about how her work was composed using the elements of sociocultural context, critical self-reflection, the body, self-other interaction, and ethics. Consider the transformative quality of performing your own words.

In considering the lived experiences that Amanda, Anthony, Trenton, Meggie, and so many students chose to engage, surely, performative embodiment is not to be taken lightly. The body in performance is not to be taken lightly because "a piece of paper, whatever the reason, can't carry the weight of a body" (4), as Elyse Pineau (2000) deftly articulates. In the performance studies classroom, one learns just how much a body weighs when re-presenting racial violence or abortion. We live in our bodies, learn about self, others, and culture through analyzing the performances of our bodies in the world. The performing body is at once a pool of data, a collector of data, and then the interpreter of data in knowledge creation, in the process of epistemology. Performance is not lightly about donning a hat or coat or costume, or turning one's back to the audience to indicate that one is not "in the scene." These are performance strategies and although relevant, mean nothing when the body itself is not engaged as an agent of embodied knowledge. Madison's thick description of performative embodiment provides focus:

> Like good theory, performance is a blur of meaning, language, and a bit of pain. Whirling past, faster than I can catch up. Testing me, often refuting me, pulling away and moving toward me. I'm almost there with it. I hold on. I keep my hands on the performance and my eyes on the theory. I am playful, but I am not playing. I do not appreciate carelessness. I pay attention. I do not let go or look away, because I have learned that all the meanings, languages, and bit of pain will come into clarity and utility like a liberation song. I need this clarity for the ones I love. (2006, 245)

Embodied performance can be a liberation song within the violence, loss, and confusion of our personal/political lives when engaged as a studied praxis of research, meaning, language, and pain. "When the students in the course," writes Joni L. Jones of her own performance pedagogy, "take on cultures they believe are other than their own, they expand themselves through the bodily incorporation that is performance" (2002, 176). Being vulnerable to the process of performance, or privy to its transformative possibilities means full engagement of the body and/in theory.

Judith Hamera refers to "body building" as the process of recognizing how we live in and make meaning through our bodies (2002, 122). For example, how is the body a part of, or held apart from, particular social practices based on race, gender, geography, religion? How do we, as Butler (2005) suggests, give an account of ourselves through performance? How then, Hamera asks, does the social construction of the body impact the meaning making process, and meaning made through performance in the classroom? I will never be pulled over for "driving while black," but Anthony has been, and most likely will continue to be. So what is the body building process he goes through to explicate that experience, to articulate those meanings in performance, particularly within the still largely traditional pedagogical separation between mind and body? Performance surely intervenes in this faux separation as performance itself is the enactment of scholarly analysis of text and/or culture. And though performance foundationally includes the body in knowledge construction, Hamera cautions against romanticizing this meeting of the mind and body lest we think of this joining as a "eureka" moment which may apolitically sanitize knowledge of the complex power structures and constraints upon everyday embodied existence, undercutting the central aim of performative autoethnography and performative-I embodiment (Spry 2006, 2010). Though being pulled over because of skin color may be a "eureka" moment for a white audience, this action is grossly mundane in Anthony's racial lived experience.

Hamera's caution moves us further into an understanding of what is personally/politically at stake in engaging the interventionist critical imagination, the "intellectual rebellion" of performance without proper methodological preparation. She writes, "It is paramount to me to explore what knowledges we think we are restoring.... I believe it can frame how we, as embodied educational subjects, survive and what we survive" (2002, 129–130), especially, I would argue, when engaging the focused, structured, theoretically grounded critical reflection of performative autoethnography. So how does the performer approach embodiment and the vulnerability required to survive? How do we engage the risk of putting our bodies on the line in performance?

Practiced Vulnerability as Agency

Growing out of a critical imagining of performative autoethnography and 15 years of trial and error pedagogy in my classroom is a process of *practiced vulnerability* (Spry 2010a). This process is designed to assist the performer in moving into embodiment of the performative-I persona. Usually in the classroom, this constitutes the first time a student has engaged in a focused, structured, theoretically grounded critical reflection and construction of a transformative experience in his life. Also, it is most likely the first time that the student has put his body on the line in performance. Long before students decide what they want to compose and perform, they must be made aware of the risks involved and thus, the vulnerability required to compose and to perform critical autoethnography.

Many exercises in the classroom focus on a *practiced vulnerability,* a methodology of moving out of one's comfort zone of familiarity, a strategic surrendering into a space of risk, of uncomfortability, of uncertainty that one experiences when critically reflecting upon and then embodying one's own experience. Practiced vulnerability is a purposeful movement into the liminality—the betwixt and betweenness—of the critical creative process of moving from person to persona. When speaking of the body in performative writing, Pelias asserts, "It offers a vulnerable self, exposed, presented bare for its personal and social curative value, for its articulation of a site for identification, and for its power as political intervention" (2007, 185). As in the composition process, practiced vulnerability does not leave the performer exposed, but rather opened to the strength gained through critical reflection. To be in this space "presented bare" is to experience a letting go of fixed meanings of long held familial and societal beliefs and values that a student has never considered critically, constituting a practiced, considered move out of one's comfort zone.

Here, letting go of fixed meanings does not mean rejecting or discarding one's established belief systems for the purpose of replacing them with others. Nor does it mean that one is overexposing oneself emotionally in ways that would embarrass. Letting go and metaphorically presented bare constitutes an expansion of self into the autoethnographic text; it is the threshold into the textualizing body where body, page, and stage animate one another expanding the epistemological possibilities of performative autoethnography.

> Describe what it might feel like to be vulnerable in the creative process. Share these descriptions in small groups. Then, as a group, describe what might be gained through a practiced vulnerability.

Practiced vulnerability also operates as a threshold into a performative-I persona. As often occurs when one first engages critical theory, there may be frustration, even a sadness, that we are unable and/or unwilling to return to a less socioculturally complicated reality, unable to see the world through a gloss or glaze of ignorance. Students continually remark, however, that although their world is now more complex, their lives are forever changed for the better for the ability to "guide judgments and evaluations emanating from [their] discontent." It is not that one does not feel discontent before critical reflection, rather, now we can articulate these intuitive feelings and offer methods of change. We can analyze why we think what we think, manifesting a richer engagement in our personal and professional lives. Ignorance, it seems, is not bliss.

Rather than a space or a process of endings or answers, practiced vulnerability is strategic surrender to an inbetweeness of self and other, to a relation, to a letting go of a single story for the purpose of "keep[ing] my hands on the performance and my eyes on the theory." It is a space of active reflection where one inhabits the intersections of his own personal experiences with the intimate politics of others. It is the practice of being vulnerable to meaning making, to the collisions and communions of our experiences with others; it is the practice of being vulnerable to the process of becoming, of expanding into the complex self created in composing autoethnography. For example, a student in my class who I will call Rick performed an autoethnography about how his own homophobia collided with his experience of being helped out by a passerby after being robbed; Rick critically reflects upon later finding out that the good Samaritan was gay. Rick then takes us back to high school where he was one of the first people to ridicule others using homophobic slurs. It is through a practice of being vulnerable to critical self-reflection that Rick finds the agency to be accountable for the conditions of his own emergence, gaining further respect for himself and others.

With a practiced vulnerability, the performer decides to move deeper into reflecting upon what happened, what sociocultural expectations and norms served to silence or inhibit his voice; or what ones did he perpetuate at the expense of others. In his performance of "Driving While Black," Anthony puts us in the car with him as he jumps into the backseat of an Escalade driven by an African-American friend in Little Jamaica in NYC. It is late in the evening, they are laughing, talking, listening to music. And then. And then Anthony narratively stops time as he and his friends see the lights of a police car in the rear view mirror. The driver had done nothing wrong, had not disobeyed any street lights, traffic signs, or cross walks. Anthony allowed himself, and performatively us, to move deep into that defining moment, into the complexities of racial construction, of fear, of power structures, and of masculinity as he narrated his body's reaction to the lights in the mirror and critique of the events that ensued, events that are, to be sure, made grotesquely mundane due to a frequency of racial profiling.

Rather than a linear path from page to stage, performance is a dialogic space where experience and text affect and are affected by one another. As the performer articulates experience through language, the language turns back upon itself—changing, redefining, breaking, and remaking the performer's understanding of the negotiation between self, other, and context within the transformative experience. Body and word, experience and craft are simultaneously reformulating meaning, revealing possibilities for usually subaltern understanding of self in the world. A practiced vulnerability is not a binary or linear process of replacing one fixed meaning for another; rather it is a space of exploration, understanding, and continual critical reflection.

Thus, one does not invite a student to enter these spaces lightly or to stumble into this process without strategy, without method, without a practiced vulnerability so that Anthony, and Amanda and Trenton can decide through their own agency what and when and how they would do this telling, this negotiated meaning, this strategic surrendering, so that they decide the weight of their body on the page and its dialogical engagement on the stage. It is a practice in being vulnerable to living in one's body when that body may be viewed as abject, abnormal, unsociable, unruly. A practiced vulnerability enables the realization that the performer, the agent in representation, is responsible for and answerable to her representation of others in the autoethnographic context.

A practiced vulnerability provides the possibility for a substantive embodiment where the student does not leave the classroom or rehearsal feeling exposed by inappropriate self-disclosure, but rather strengthened by embodying her own critical reflection upon lived experience crafted from her own wisdom and use of theory. In Meggie Mapes's "Yet To Name," she practiced a vulnerability that allowed her to open herself up to the *many* sides of the terribly polarized debates surrounding abortion. In this way she was able to inhabit feelings and experiences and research connected to the events that perhaps would not have been understood and articulated. Being vulnerable to the difficulties of the experience allowed Meggie to craft a story, a *wisdom* that we all learn from no matter where we stand in relation to this intense issue.

Words can construct, but cannot hold the weight of the body. But a practiced vulnerability might assist in the kind of "body building" needed for the strength in understanding "how and what we survive."

Who and What Are We Performing in Performative Autoethnography?

I love performance most when I enter into it, when it calls me forward shamelessly, across those hard-edged maps into spaces where I must go, terrains that are foreign, scary, uninhabitable, but necessary. I must go to them to know myself more, to know you more.

D. Soyini Madison,
"Performing Theory/Embodied Writing," 244

Upon initially thinking about performing autoethnography, one may think, "If I am performing my own writing, why worry about embodiment or rehearsal? I embody myself in my everyday life. I don't need to prepare to perform *myself.*" Performing self in front of an audience is, I would argue, the most "foreign, scary, [seemingly] uninhabitable, but necessary" kind of performance because self is, perhaps, the most difficult text to embody. The first time I performed a work that I had written, "Skins: A Daughter's (Re)Construction of Cancer," I had never felt so vulnerable in my 20 years of performance work (Spry 1997). It remains one of the most profound experiences in my life due to what I learned about the effects of sociocultural expectations and my understanding of the connections between self/other/context/language. What I learned about cancer, gender, my mother, and grief by embodying my own critical reflection upon the experience shook me to my core. As many students say after performing autoethnography, I was never the same after that.

> Describe yourself as the performer of your text. Now describe yourself as the persona in the text. What parts of the persona will be easy to embody, which parts will be difficult?

Self as Persona

As we move into thinking about who we are performing when performing autoethnography, consider another excerpt from "Paper and Skin: Bodies of Loss and Life":

Delivery. The only cure for me. Delivering the body. Delivering the story. We would both die if he were not born. He would die regardless. Too young to live. Too small. Too soon. No decision. To live or die. No decision except delivering the story of my son.

there is something about putting it here
on stage
with you,
something about being torn apart
in front of you
that makes it matter
differently...

Maybe it's because when I am here on stage with you performing autoethnography, the "I" is not me, Scheckner's "not-not-me," the person I am here/now is me twice removed—once through writing, and again through performance. She is me the autobiographical artifact, the self-representational persona. "I" am/is not real, but a representation released by postmodernity from any ties, Sidonie Smith might say, "to a convenient secure anchorage of 'selfhood' [or] an unproblemitized 'experience'" (39). "I" am so mediated by language, culture, morays of textuality, and conventions of performance—who the hell knows who I/we am/are?

Maybe that's why I lay my torn-a-parts here on stage with you, because this fictional representational context of the stage, is the only safe space to admit that the only "truth" is the ficticity of self and experience; within the constructs of grief and loss, being cut loose from a modernist romantic version of life and death is a relief. Here, my body can be a fish. I can invite you to consider that my nails are the fish scales, because, after watching my ashes ride down a river, my body can no longer live on the earth. Here truth matters, differently.

In the autoethnographic text, you are performing a self (a *you*) that you constructed; that *self is a persona* that you will seek to embody in performance. There are, in a sense, *two* complex constructions of self occurring in performing performative autoethnography; there are you the *persona* and you the *performer*. The *persona* is the crafted articulation, a critical construction of self—of you—*as she/ you exist in the story*. This persona is the self that exists in the particular times and places of the autoethnographic text, the self carefully constructed through agency and representation, by the elements for composing performative autoethnography; it is the self created from the courage to be vulnerable to critical reflection. "Performing narrative," writes Langellier and Peterson, "is not a discrete event—somehow external to the body—of processing and recounting prior events" (2004, 9). The self created on the page through intense critical reflection is, in a sense, you and not you at once. As discussed in chapter 1, self is heterogeneous, multidimensional, fragmented. "The persona I am here/now is me twice removed—once through writing and again through performance." Through engaging a performative-I disposition in the writing of autoethnography, you have created a performative-I persona in the autoethnography, a version of you created through the theory/method praxis of performative autoethnography.

Self as Performer

The *performer* is *you*—the self that is seeking to embody the persona in the text through performance. In the above excerpt from "Paper and Skin," I reflect upon the feeling, the location, the process of moving between performer and persona. As in the textualizing body, where body/self, page/text, and stage/performance are interdependent upon one another in the construction of meaning, so are performer and persona dialogically interdependent upon one another for performance. In "Paper and Skin," consider how the performer and persona comment upon, *depend upon* one another in conceptualizing and constructing the autoethnography. The performer does not leave herself behind in order to embody the persona; rather the performer is in a constant process of interpreting the text in her effort to embody the persona. This interpretation process is the foundation of the elements of an embodied performance presented later in this chapter.

Performative-I Persona

Performer and persona are in a constant process of knowing, being, becoming, of (re)introducing one to oneself. The embodiment process is one of continual *becoming* where we learn more about ourselves and others through embodying the language chosen to represent experience (Deleuze and Guattari 2009). In performing autoethnography, the pedagogical process intensifies as, through performance, you are continually seeking to become *a performative-I persona*, a persona, though crafted, critiqued, and considered, that is still in flux, heterogeneous, always in progress of negotiating a self/other/context/language relation. In other words, through performing the persona I created in "Paper and Skin," I continue to work through and understand the grief and healing process in ways available only through writing and performance. Thus, one must not make the mistake of thinking that since this is one's story, it does not need intense rehearsal for the stage.

Ultimately, during performance the audience should see, for example, Tami the *persona* as she exists in "Paper and Skin," rather than Tami the *person* as she might exist in daily life. I must answer the question, "Who am I in the context of this experience?" The Meggie we see in "Yet To Name" is different from the Meggie sitting in class; she must answer the question of who she has constructed in the autoethnography and then seek to live into that version or part of herself; *this is the essence of embodiment*. In *Performing Narrative* Langellier and Peterson argue that the body cannot

> be reduced to thought and consciousness. Performing narrative is not a cognitive or reflective process for which the body is a container.... Before performing narrative is conceived or represented, it is lived through the body as meaningful. Our task is to explicate the context of relations in which the body is both part and participant. (2004, 9)

Wallace Bacon (1979) refers to this process of "explicating the context of relations" as *matching* the body in the text with the body of the performer. This may seem an already "perfect match." However, "the body is not a container"; in performative autoethnography we are making meaning, making sense of a transformative, challenging, perhaps difficult and confusing experience in our lives. We are constructing another dimension of our subjectivity, another component of our collective identity. We are *doing* meaning, making the performative-I persona. "Narrative performance," write Langellier and Peterson, "materializes performativity in that 'experiential moment' of learning something about oneself and the world. A risky and dangerous negotiation between a doing and a thing done" (2004, 3). Composing the autoethnographic text may be the first time you have thought *critically* about who you are with others in terms of race, class, gender, etc. The body on the page, the body in performative autoethnography, is not always a perfect or easy match with our construction of self in everyday life. This is why a practiced vulnerability is so important in rehearsal to effect dialogic engagement between person and persona.

In seeking to embody the performative-I persona, you begin to reclaim creative intuitive knowledge. Intuitive knowing is the epistemology of felt-sensing, of knowing when something "feels right." It is how we learned language as children; it is how we know when we love or dislike someone; it is an internal knowledge that an entrepreneur or inventor believes in. It is part of the creative/critique/culture frame of the performance studies classroom.

Because the body, page, and stage are interdependent, *the process of embodiment will change the written text.* As you try on the words of the text, your body and the language you created for/from your body will transform one another as you engage the process of becoming the persona, of matching bodies. This is the engagement of the textualizing body. As you begin to speak the text in rehearsal, some words will move with your body's understanding of the experience, some will not. This is Gingrich-Philbrook's (2001) notion of body-language-body-language at work. It is the always continuing development of your relationship to and with words as ethical agent representing experience. Your embodiment of language through performance foregrounds and intensifies this relationship. It is the ongoing work of the "articulate body" (Pineau 2000), the textualizing body, the body's experience of trying on and rearranging socially constructed meanings of words, the process of the body seeking to articulate meaning through language.

The articulate body implies agency, an influence with language of how and what will be said. But the textualizing body also works hard to fit in with the sociocultural molds created by words articulating dominant cultural norms. Revealing and investigating this process of give and take between ourselves and how we represent ourselves and others through language is the pedagogical nexus of performance, and is made further salient through performative auto-ethnography. Thus, the textualizing body in performance is a body that continually accounts for its sociocultural emergence through the performance choices on stage.

Clearly, embodying a performative-I persona requires a clear and rigorous method of rehearsal and performance. As performer, I go to the person on the page "to know myself more, to know you more" (Madison 2006). And yet this is never a linear process from page to stage, from word to body, from one to another. The writing, rehearsal, and performance process is always turning in on itself, looking forward and back, being transformed by the constant conversation of being and becoming. Though I have been performing for over 30 years and have performed, for example, "Paper and Skin" many times, each time—and each performative-I persona—is decidedly different due to the divergences in myself, others, and our worlds since the last performance.

Questions for Further Consideration

1. Consider Conquergood's (2004) conceptualizations of performance as analysis, artistry, and articulation. Explain how each of these is realized through performative autoethnography.

2. Explain how a practiced vulnerability can help critical reflection.

3. Explain the difference between performer and persona in autoethnography.

Chapter Five

Stage
Embodying Performative Autoethnography

As we move into the performing body, consider D. Soyini Madison's earlier words in relation to a student's writing for autoethnographic performance:

> Like good theory, performance is a blur of meaning, language, and a bit of pain. Whirling past, faster than I can catch up. Testing me, often refuting me, pulling away and moving toward me. I'm almost there with it. I hold on. I keep my hands on the performance and my eyes on the theory. I am playful, but I am not playing. I do not appreciate carelessness. I pay attention. I do not let go or look away, because I have learned that all the meanings, languages, and bits of pain will come into clarity and utility like a liberation song. I need this clarity for the ones I love. (2006, 245)

"Tats" by Zeb Scanlan, from "Through the Earlobe"

My flesh, like the flesh of others is not only the plastic wrap of my physique but also a canvas, an empty room, a blank surface ready to be covered in images that supposedly mean something or symbolize an aspect of life. The other 96% of my skin that remains blank awaits the delightful sting of a needle dripping with ink, syrupy, silken, jet-black ink. My fleshy saran coat deserves to be decorated with meaningful intricacies and silvery, pierced punctuation. I am the Salvador Dali of my somatic embodiment.

My tattoo has a face; I believe the human face, in all of its sharp muscularity can be more expressive than any words. I believe in the human face. My tattoo mimics, symbolizes, critiques, imitates and evaluates the sun and the sun is the closest thing to a god that any living, conscious human being will ever conceive.

A young man's face will tell you much more than the words he gives you after you ask him "what does it take to be a man?" and the muscular reaction in a young woman's face will say much more than what she can vocalize after you ask her "What does it take to be smart, when all they want is beautiful?" A facial expression can lay all the pieces down right in front of you. The face can tell more than words and the sun keeps us alive. The sun, beating down with searing endearment, like a mother that only visits during the day, that's okay, let the night wash all my obligations away. The impending clearance of some false appearance should not, cannot, will not exist in my mind. Be all you can be without pulling a trigger.

My body resists the sluggish lifestyle of some tradition-ridden, fast food munching so-called American who is plagued with surplus repression and the idea that they have ideals. I refuse to stand idle on a cold porch like a scarecrow huffing in the fumes of some corporate conglomerate while saying to all the naysayers, "I'm gonna die anyway" or "you gotta die somehow." Don't try to tell me what for while sucking off on some nicotine knob of commercial candy. I couldn't hear you through all the smacking; the only noise coming through your teeth is the squelching sound of something fast and fried, something greasy-wet and extra-sized, get some exercise. Food that's fast is only a last resort in my world. "It's cheap and it tastes so good," that doesn't mean you need to drive on over to KentuckyMcBurgerFriedKing and gobble down another fix for cardiac arrest.

Steve, the big, bald man with the prosthetic nose drew something on my shoulder after I flipped through many pages and told him what I wanted. Hmm, I think I think I'll have… that one. Like a child choosing their favorite flavor of ice cream while at the same time like a soldier accepting some honorable decoration. The noisy, hectic, alive and well streets of Dublin outside awaited my first brandishing under an Irish sun. First I wanted a biohazard symbol filled with Celtic knots scribbled across my ribcage, but Steve said I might pass out from the piercing pain of not having had any experience underneath the needle. I think I would've been alright but I obliged and accepted his theory. "You walk right out if they don't use clean, brand new needles," he wanted me to remember this especially. Practice hygiene, cuz if the needle ain't clean, the tattoo remains unseen. And with a trace here, a scribble there and wipe across my arm, my shoulder remained inked.

Well it has to mean something, I thought, as I walked out the door with my new, bleeding tattoo. I knew it did, but I just couldn't pin point it. Well the sun is cool and has to do with nature and… I like nature. That works, that's what I'll tell people, good enough, whatever. Definitions aren't everything, but that one was a little frail, it needed some substance and meat and through the daily introspection and occasional epiphanies I have from time to time, the ink seemed to define itself and I realized what my tattoo really stands for. Underneath the sun as a crying baby a naked infant, I was cradled and raised by my father's dark hands up above the earth. In the middle of a forest I was held under the brightest star in the galaxy latching on to the natural world, my existence unfurled, as I became one organism with the earth. The sun looking down upon me, accepting my father's presentation of his newborn son.

My tattoo smells like a fallen oak tree burning under the full sun. The color the pain the needle brought was like the sound of burning coals, the noise of oil burning through a giant steel ship, sinking into the freezing depths of the ocean. My tattoo sees the hawk flying horizontally with the setting sun and hears the dark color of an owl's glare, perched up above the forest, and feels the darkness of night that surrounds the full moon. All these senses thrown into a blender and then splattered on the wall; do not break my fall; because once I get up, I'll only be stronger. My sense of smell thicker, my vision sharper, my eardrums tight, loose, tight, catching all the sounds of a developing, of an evolving, of an always-learning life. (this is the entire unpublished text)

Though we cannot see his physical performance as it occurred on stage, we can feel the movement of the body in performance as it is written on the page. Look again at Madison's passage beginning the chapter; one can feel the "blur of meaning" in Zeb Scanlan's performance. He is playful but not playing. His critique of consumerism testing him as much as the audience. The "bit of pain" from his tattoo pulls us in and through and with the performing body making this a clear example of a textualizing body.

So as we move our hands toward performance and our eyes toward theory, we will move into our methodology for performing autoethnography.

Elements of an Embodied Performance

The elements of composing performative autoethnography have provided the necessary foundation in conceptualizing and applying agency and representation in writing. These same principles of empowerment through agency and accountability through representation are the foundation for the choices made in constructing performance. Perhaps even more salient than writing, performance is a process of *representation,* carrying with it all of the rights and responsibility for empowerment and accountability that are the core of performative autoethnographic writing. "Performance," writes Conquergood, "sometimes resists, exceeds, and overwhelms the constraints and strictures of writing" (1991, 193).

The method of composing performative autoethnography moves the researcher from the somatic, the knowledge and experience of the body, to the semantic, the linguistic representation of that knowledge. Now in moving deeper into the body-language-body-language praxis, this method of performing autoethnography will ask the researcher to go from the semantic, the language on the page, to the somatic, interpreting that language in and through the body, matching and coalescing language-body, becoming the "Salvador Dali of my somatic embodiment" as Scanlan playfully suggests.

Here, then, is a methodological process of moving the performer into the autoethnographic text, in concert with Pineau's assertion that "performance methodology means the rigorous, systematic exploration-through-enactment of real and imagined experience in which learning occurs through sensory awareness and kinesthetic engagement" (2002, 50). The elements of embodied performance is a rigorous and systematic methodology that I use in my performance studies classes and is informed by the rich history in performance studies of comprehensive methodologies for interpreting and embodying a text for performance (Bacon 1979, Bell 2008, Long and Hopkins 1997, Pelias and Stevenson 2008).

Note that the methodology offered here is also applicable for the embodiment of personae other than self. In my performative autoethnography courses, along with creating their own persona, students are required to perform a persona other than themselves for at least one minute of the total performance time of the autoethnography. These persona would emerge out of the autoethnography—often out of the self-other interaction element of composition—in the form of someone who played a significant role in the story. This embodiment of another assists the performer in understanding the implications of representation through performance.

Artistic Work Ethic

Along with theoretic understanding of performance and performative autoethnography, the only other ingredient required for this method is hard work and commitment to the performance process. I do not view performance as a magically spontaneous process that will simply occur when one is waiting for one's muse. *Art is hard work*, and as illustrated in discussions of embodiment, it requires the labor of analysis and preparation in rehearsal.

I do not believe in the concept of talent in my classroom. Performance is a difficult and risky process which requires commitment to the emotional and physical obligations necessary to embody the complexity of a persona. Everyone is capable of hard work; *everyone* is capable of performance. Like any other method in the humanities and sciences, performance is a method of inquiry, of learning, of understanding. One cannot solve a proof in math without doing the labor of mathematic methods, or make scientific discoveries without understanding biology, or write without doing the work of sentence structure and grammar. As Conquergood contends, "Performance is based in activism, outreach, connection to community, to projects that reach outside the academy and are rooted in an ethic of reciprocity and exchange, and as such, generates knowledge that is tested by practice within a community" (2004, 318). Performance director and activist Augosto Boal, for example, works with people around the world, actors and non-actors, for the purpose of social change.

Both my mother and father grew up in a working class environment. I am a first-generation college student. My mother's side of the family were union members. I was raised on the axiom that hard work is the measure of a person, an ethic of character. As a musician for 25 years, my dad always told me that success "in the business" was 99 percent hard work; the same applies in the business of creating knowledge through performance. During my PhD work at Southern Illinois University at Carbondale, as I was writing my dissertation and freaking out about my future (or lack thereof) in academia, one of my professors in performance studies said, "Just do good work." I've never forgotten this advice and have found it to be simply and profoundly accurate both personally and professionally.

So, with the life blood of good theory and the courage to be vulnerable, let's do good work in performance. Offering a tangible and systematic method of approaching and engaging performative autoethnography, elements of an embodied performance include dialogical performance, internal/external dichotomy, and performance choices.

Dialogical Performance

Surely, presence of and interconnectedness to others is foundational to dialogue. In "Paper and Skin," I write about the grief process and subsequent depression as the inability to create or feel dialogic engagement of any kind really. In speaking of Dwight Conquergood's concept of dialogical performance, Madison writes, "Dialogue is framed as performance to emphasize the living communion of a felt-sensing, embodied interplay and engagement between human beings" (2005, 9). Becoming aware of the deeply fundamental presence and necessity of performative dialogue in autoethnographic research moved me into a different understanding of the negotiated interconnectedness of selves and others in contexts. Any innocence I had about research (and life) had left my body after our loss; fragmentation of self and spirit did not bring about the absence of dialogue, rather it foregrounded its inherent presence.

In his mapping of ethical challenges in performing ethnography, which formed the basis of ethics in the elements of composing autoethnography in chapter 3, Conquergood offers *dialogical performance* as the ethical process of engaging the other in performance (1985). At its core, dialogical performance is the ethical engagement of the other, or persona, for the purpose of an on-going embodied collaboration of learning. Dialogical performance is the foundation of the textualizing body. What follows are main ideas in the depth and breadth of disciplinary conceptualizations in performance studies of dialogical performance.

> ▷ *A performer's fundamental interest is the dialogue that takes place between self and the text in rehearsal, and between persona and the audience in performance.* The performer is seeking dialogue with the self/persona constructed in the autoethnography. A deep and different kind of learning of the complexity of self-other-culture begins through this process.

☞ *Dialogical performance embraces and complicates diversity, difference, and pluralism* (Madison 2005). In seeking a complex understanding of difference through dialogical performance, facile approaches and obsequious nods toward "diversity" are quickly and clearly abandoned for dialogue that embraces the paradox of difference and unity, for agreement and disagreement (9). This is the basis of composing performative autoethnography; now, in performing autoethnography, one works to embody these embrasures and complications somatically.

☞ *Dialogical performance does not require agreement, only that each seek to understand each other* (Conquergood 1985). As we are often at odds with parts of ourselves, the performer may be at odds with parts of her autoethnography; she may believe ethically in a part of the text, but still be coming to terms with meaning she has made about parts of the experience. This is where dialogical performance operates in a practiced vulnerability. In "From Goldilocks to Dreadlocks" it was difficult for me to embody my own lack of responsibility in and perpetuation of racism.

☞ *The first task in dialogical performance is textual analysis, interpreting what is being communicated in the text, making meaning of the text.* As we will encounter, the performer will analyze his text to create performance choices.

☞ *Performers hear, in the most profound sense, another voice, suggesting an engaged self interacting with another, making an imaginative leap into another world* (Pelias 1992). The autoethnographic performer begins to hear the voice of his words, of his negotiated critical reflection, in the process of becoming. To hear one's words spoken, resonating in the body, dialoging with one's own subjectivities through embodiment is a profoundly moving process in understanding self and other.

☞ *To engage in an intimate merger between self and other/text is the ultimate goal of dialogical performance* (Pelias 1992). The autoethnographic performer engages a practiced vulnerability, seeking an embodied becoming, a coalesced matching of body and language, a realization of the performative-I persona.

☞ *The performer recognizes similarities and differences, embodying comparisons and contrasts.* One does not ever *fully know* self or other through performing autoethnography; such would be hubris rather than pedagogy. Performance is not that innocent. Rather, it is through performance that I come to know more fully the comparisons and contrasts, the painful and liberating process of representing the intimate nuances of a "hermeneutics of experience, relocation, copresence, humility, and vulnerability" that Dwight Conquergood (1991) describes, where knowledge is located, engaged, and "forged from *solidarity with*, not separation from, the people" in research (Spry 2006, 315). This is assuming, of course, that people would desire forging knowledge together; and, if not, that the autoethnographer has the humility to recognize resistance to collaboration and the courage to critically reflect upon why the resistance exists, and then to embody this complexity in performance.

☞ *A commitment to dialogue [in performance] insists on keeping alive the inter-animating tension between Self and Other. It resists closure and totalizing domination of a single viewpoint, unitary system of thought* (Conquergood 1992, 11). Performance does not offer the definitive representation of autoethnographic experience and interaction, but rather continues the ongoing engagement of making meaning in one's negotiation with self/other/culture/language.

Dialogical performance, then, is the interpretation of the complex interaction between performer (self), text (other), and sociocultural context; it is what allows/invites/motivates an audience to engage the performance, to communicate with the persona, to exist in the world of the story. It is the space of intimate engagement between audience and performance, the space of intimate pedagogy where audience members can feel, see, and experience a story that encourages them to generate meaning of related experiences in their own lives. Perhaps they begin to reflect upon their own or others' acts of racism or activism; or they see that they are not alone in experiencing assault, or that there are many forms of grief. They see that there is more than just a single story.

> Write a paragraph explaining what you believe is the most important part of dialogical performance. Get into groups and share your writing.

The more deeply engaged the performer is in dialogical performance, the more deeply engaged the audience is in the performance and, thus, the pedagogical process. Remember that the disciplinary goal in performance studies is engaged pedagogy, *learning from and in performance*. Dialogical performance is why we do performative autoethnography.

Preparing for Rehearsal

- *Begin the performance process by working from the best draft of the performative autoethnography.* Though the text will change as you begin to embody the language, you must have a typed best-draft version to begin rehearsal.

- *Approach all rehearsals through a practiced vulnerability,* an openness to the agency of vulnerability in the embodiment of your performative autoethnography.

🖝 *Find a of room of your own.* Performers must find a space of privacy where no one will be walking through or needing access. In the beginning process of embodiment, of moving from performer to persona, the performer will feel odd, silly, and very uncomfortable trying on the voice and body of the persona in the text, even though it is a version of her own. You need a space where you can safely move out of your comfort zone and into persona. And btw, turn off the cell phone and computer.

Internal/External Dichotomy

Performance methods are concerned with *what* is said (the text) and *how* to say it (performance choices). The internal/external dichotomy comprises the operational basis of the *what* and *how* of doing performance. When something is dichotomous, it means that two separate things have interdependently engaged one another to make something *other*, something different than the two original substances. In the elements of an embodied performance, the internal elements (thoughts, feelings, attitudes, and emotions) and the external elements (voice, body, and space) are dichotomous; they work together to create an embodied persona.

The internal and external dichotomy are similar to performance studies scholar Wallace Bacon's concept of the inner form and outer form of literature when seeking to embody the other (or persona) through the performance of poetry. He writes:

What the interpreter [performer] does...is to establish some congruence between the inner form of the poem and his own inner self (working backward and forward between the poem and himself), and then to embody the poem—literally giving body to the experience—so that through his own outer form (his voice, his countenance, his body) he in a sense becomes the poem. The poem now becomes audible and visible—and if the interpreter succeeds in establishing congruence between the inner form of the poem and his own inner form...the poem will come alive, will have presence." (1979, 37)

The autoethnographic performer, then, seeks to embody congruence between the inner form of her writing and the inner form of her self, constituting the process of becoming the performative-I persona. The textualizing body engages experience, autoethnographic text, and now, the performance/embodiment of the text.

Like Bacon's inner and outer form, *the internal and external elements are gleaned through textual analysis* of the performative auto-ethnography. Remember that even though this autoethnography was written by you, it is a carefully constructed version of you created for a particular purpose and a particular story. The analysis of the text moves you from performer to persona, from performative-I disposition

> Find a particular moment in your text. What are the internal elements in that moment? Now concentrate on feeling these elements while speaking/embodying the words in the text.

to performative-I persona; one can only make this transformation through analysis. Based on the language of the text, the performer considers the mix and complexity of internal elements that might be present in a persona who is speaking the particular words in the time and space of the text. Then, based on this analysis of internal elements (thoughts, feelings, attitudes, and emotions) of the persona, the performer decides how the internal elements would manifest themselves through voice and body (external elements), as well as how performance space might be used to illustrate or extend the meaning of the text.

It is in this process of analysis of one's own text that the autoethnographer/performer moves deeper into a critical understanding of the experience. As you analyze what internal elements are manifested from the text, the text itself becomes more refined as words, phrases, scenes are more intimately engaged through dialogical performance. Through this process, you will be able to engage and challenge your writing on a deeper level. Performance allows us to engage the body created through writing, to dialogically engage and perform the self negotiated through the performative-I disposition of writing. The body, word, and performance are animated by one another in the textualizing body. And so in trying on this body of words, there will necessarily be parts that fit and parts that do not. You will know this intuitively, through a performance-sensitive way of knowing.

So, although the text will be somewhat in flux as the body and word continue to know one another within the textualizing body, one must, of course at some point, decide *what* is being said and *how* it is manifested in movement and voice onstage. These decisions are called *performance choices*. These choices move you from the performative-I disposition in writing to the performative-I persona in performance.

Methodology Overview

INTERNAL ELEMENTS ⟷ EXTERNAL ELEMENTS

= PERFORMANCE CHOICES

Though the internal elements are analyzed first, the connection between internal and external elements is continually interactive, transactional, and interdependent. As indicated in the two-way arrow, performance choices are gleaned through an interactive, back-and-forth engagement between the internal (thoughts, feelings, attitudes, emotions) and external (voice, body, and space) elements. Feeling internal elements in a gesture or body movement may then refine or redefine the internal element in the back-and-forth movement between them. Use these elements as goals and guidelines for your rehearsal and performance process.

Step One: Analyzing Internal Elements

1. The internal elements include thoughts, feelings, attitudes, and emotions.

    a. They are the interior interactions of the persona, or the inner form of the text. *These interior interactions are communicated to an audience through the voice and body of the persona, or the external elements, constituting performance choices.*

    b. This process is directly synonymous with the process of communication where we can never know exactly what someone is thinking or feeling; we have only the *what* (the language) and the *how* (how it is said) to understand one another.

    c. So, the performer must interpret/analyze the persona's internal elements before deciding how to communicate these elements through voice and body.

    d. *The more complex and specific the interpretation of the internal and external elements, the more complex, specific, and thus, dialogically compelling is the performance.*

2. Analyzing the internal elements is somewhat tricky for the autoethnographic performer, as he must analyze the internal elements *of the persona in the text* rather than how he, the *performer, may feel about the text.* These are two different things; it is the difference between *persona* (how/who you are in the text) and *performer* (how you feel about the text), and foregrounds the necessity for the performer to think of the text as a specific subjectivity or construction of self.

3. Each scene or fragment or narrative section of the text must be carefully and thoughtfully analyzed.

    a. What were you feeling during each part of the experience?

    b. BE SPECIFIC. It is not enough to think "sad" or "happy";

rather, think sad or happy how? why? with whom? What are the circumstances?

c. What, where, and why are the *conflicting* internal elements? Autoethnographic texts are based upon conflicting ideas and emotions as we work toward giving an account of ourselves. For example, in Mapes's performance of "Yet To Name," she had to embody the conflict she felt before and after the medical procedure.

d. Dialogic performance requires that you embody the specific internal elements of the text for the audience to be able to dialogically engage the performance. The more specific the internal elements, the more compelling the performance.

e. *Brainstorm* various lists of internal elements based on different fragments and scenes within the text. Use these lists in rehearsal.

4. What are the thoughts, feelings, attitudes, and emotions when speaking to a *particular audience* about an experience? When do they change? Where? Why?

5. Create a *map of internal elements* for the persona.

a. This map charts the emotional, attitudinal, etc., changes and transitions in the text.

b. Using a double or triple spaced script of the autoethnography, write the internal elements directly above the lines of the text. Note that these will change/refine/redefine as you move deeper into the embodiment of the text through rehearsal, *as you get to know the you who is the performative-I persona.*

6. As the internal elements of the persona begin to take shape, they then are used as the basis for deciding upon the external elements (voice, body, and space) of the persona, or the performance choices.

**Step Two: Connecting Internal and External Elements
for Performance Choices**

1. Decisions about what to do with the voice and body of the
   persona, and how to use space within the performance are
   called *performance choices*. Performance choices manifest the
   embodiment of the text.

   INTERNAL ELEMENTS ⟷ EXTERNAL ELEMENTS

   = PERFORMANCE CHOICES

   a. As the autoethnographic text comprises *what* is commu-
      nicated in performance, performance choices comprise
      how something is communicated and are based on the
      internal elements.

   b. How does the persona speak and move?

   c. How does the persona's use of space illustrate internal
      elements?

2. Performances choices must be *purposeful and intentional*.

   a. There must be a *purpose or intention* for all choices of voice,
      body, and space. Otherwise, the words, the language spo-
      ken by the persona will not seem to "fit" the voice, body
      movements, facial expressions.

   b. The purpose and intention of performance choices—tone
      or rate of the voice, the gestures or expressions of the
      persona—are decided and motivated by the internal ele-
      ments of the text.

3. Performance choices must be clear and specific.

   a. As in communication, we cannot read the mind (the
      internal elements) of whom we are communicating with.
      We rely on interpreting *what* is said (the words) and *how* it
      is said (performance choices), thus the audience must be
      able to engage clear and specific performance choices to
      make meaning of the autoethnographic text.

b. The degree to which the audience can dialogically engage the performance is based on the clarity of specific, detailed, and complex performance choices in voice, body, and space.

4. Performance choices must be *ethical*, grounded in dialogical performance.

  a. The same ethical principles of agency and accountability addressed in the elements of composing performative autoethnography are the foundation for the ethical choices made in constructing performance.

  b. The ethical pitfalls possible in composing performative autoethnography are also possible in performance. Review the descriptions for the ethical pitfalls and critically reflect upon whether your performance choices entail: custodian's rip-off, the blamer, the hero, the victim/survivor, enthusiast's infatuation, curator's exhibitionist (Conquergood 1985).

5. Performance choices must be allowed to *develop*.

  a. A common mistake for performers at any level is to force voice, movement, or gestures into/onto the persona.

  b. Just like the writing process, the construction of the persona in performance must be allowed to develop slowly, to change, to allow the language to move around, through, and into the body.

  c. Try to think "What am I (the persona) thinking/feeling?" rather than "How should I sound or gesture when I say this?" Performance choices must be felt inside to be manifested outside.

Step Three: Making Performance Choices of Voice, Body, Audience, and Space

1. *Use of Voice*: How does my voice, as persona, illustrate the internal elements?

   a. Voice should reflect the internal elements of the persona. (Remember that the internal elements themselves are discovered through analysis, *and will certainly change* as you continue the process of embodiment.)

   b. Changes in volume, pitch, rate are clearly motivated by specific internal elements.

      i. What do the complex internal elements *sound* like when spoken?

         For example, in embodying the fear and confusion of grief in specific parts of "Paper and Skin," I found that my voice would quicken and slow down; there were many pauses as I struggled to find words.

      ii. What internal elements of the persona motivate a fast rate of speech? Slow? Quiet? Loud?

      iii. When does the persona pause, laugh, breathe deeply, sigh?

   c. Always work toward *purposefulness and clarity* of vocal performance choices.

2. *Use of Body*: How does my body as persona, literally from head to toe, illustrate the internal elements?

   a. Just like in vocal choices, the body in performance should reflect the internal elements of the persona.

   b. The body is *always actively involved* in performance.

      i. A common mistake made by beginning performers is to "forget" that they have a body since the body is often forgotten in the traditional learning process.

    ii. The body is always "alive" with the performance choices of the persona.

c. How does the body of the persona move motivated by specific internal elements?

    i. When is the body still? Sitting? Pacing?

    ii. How does the body indicate, for example, agitation, sadness, elation? And how does this change? Why, where, with whom, and when? For example, in "Tattoo Stories," I trace the progression of events that lead to a nervous breakdown; between each part of the text I would slowly and agitatedly walk in a circle reflecting the buildup of frustration leading to the eventual breakdown.

d. How does the persona carry herself? What is her body carriage like in general? in specific moments?

    i. Straight-backed, slumped? Fidgety, slow moving?

    ii. When and how does the body carriage change?

e. Gestures are in sync with body movement.

    i. A common mistake is to force gestures upon the body rather than letting gestures grow out of body movement.

    ii. Remember, always think "What am I (the persona) thinking/feeling?" rather than "How should I gesture when I say this?"

f. The *entire* body is considered in embodiment.

    i. What do the guts feel like, knees, legs? Any of these external elements could be an anchor to the internal elements.

    ii. For example, what does it feel like for Amanda *in her guts* to feel agency and empowerment in parts of her autoethnography? How does she carry herself differently during those moments?

g. Energy, energy, energy. Whatever the choices in body movement, whether the body is very active or stock still, the body should always be energized with intention and commitment to dialogical performance. Remember, *the body is always "alive" as the persona onstage…always.* For example, in "Skins," during the "BANG BANG BANG" I chose to stand in the middle of the stage as still as possible, staring straight forward. The incongruency between my rigid body and the traumatic action spoken in text added dimension to the performance, allowing the audience to dialogically engage my mother's experience as well as my experience of her pain in that moment.

h. Variety of movement and variety of body position are clearly connected to the emotional map of the internal elements of the persona.

i. *Purposefulness and clarity* in performance choices for the body.

3. *Audience, or "to whom is the persona speaking?" focal point.* The performer must decide whom is being spoken to in the autoethnographic performance. Internal elements change due to whom the persona is speaking and how she feels about the other. What is the relationship between the persona and the audience?

a. *This decision will be indicated through the performance choice of eye contact or focal point.*

b. *General audience*: here the persona is telling the story to an unspecified group of people. There may or may not be a specific demographic or population indicated, but the persona is speaking to a group.

i. Focal point: if the performer is talking to a general

audience, then eye contact is made with the whole audience depending on the internal elements. For example, though the whole audience is being spoken to, when does Meggie in "Yet To Name" not want to make eye contact, or look away, or look directly and pointedly at the audience?

ii. This is called an open scene because the persona recognizes the existence of the present audience.

c. *Fictive other*: the autoethnography may contain a scene where the persona is speaking to a specified individual in the text (as indicated in the self-other interaction composition element), i.e. the persona might be speaking to her mother, father, friend, coach, etc. How do the internal and external elements change when talking to this person/ audience?

i. Focal point: this is called a closed scene because the actual audience is not present for the persona in this part of the performance; in other words, the audience is not part of the fictive world of the performance. The persona is making eye contact with a fictive other in the text.

ii. As the persona, the performer establishes the presence of the other person by "seeing" the fictive other. The persona must not make eye contact with the actual audience or the convention of speaking to another—the closed scene—will be disrupted.

iii. If the *performer* is committed to this performance choice, the *persona* will be speaking to a fictive other, and the audience will believe it as well.

iv. The most important thing is not that the audience actually "see" the other person, but that the audience believe that the persona sees and is communicating with the other person, what this means to the story, internal elements, etc.

d. *Self*: here the persona is speaking to herself. This may be a fragment of the autoethnography where we see the persona's internal thoughts, conflicts, joys.

   i. Focal point: This is also a closed scene where the persona's focal point clearly indicates that she is alone.

   ii. Again, because it is a closed scene, eye contact cannot be made with the actual audience.

e. *Shifting or multiple audience*: sometimes the persona will be speaking to the general audience (open scene) and then switch to a closed scene where he is speaking to a fictive other. He may then switch back to talking with the audience about what he was thinking or feeling during the closed scene conversation.

   i. Focal point: use the same focal point directions as above.

   ii. When you shift to a different focal point do it with *intention and directness*; believe it or not, the audience will quickly and easily move with the persona through these shifts.

4. *Use of Space or Staging*

a. The use of space concerns how the performance will be *staged*.

b. Staging is essential to consider no matter where the performance is occurring. This may be on a traditional stage, in a conference room, in a church basement, on a street corner, etc.

c. Staging *extends the textual analysis/interpretation/meaning of the text*.

d. Staging can be literal or metaphoric. *All use of space is defined by how the persona moves within the space.*

  i. In literal staging the persona is set in a particular place, a kitchen, living room, funeral, carnival, etc.

  ii. In metaphoric staging, space is used in abstract ways. Here, body movement defines space rather than relying completely on props and set. *For example,* a student did an autoethnography dealing with the social expectations of being the daughter of a pastor. She split the audience in half and had them sit on either side of a chalk line written on the floor. Beginning at one end and ending at the other, she did the entire performance walking on the line as if it were a tightrope. This abstract or metaphoric use of space heightened the feeling articulated in the autoethnography of being always under observation, judged, and fearing she might "fall" in the sight/minds of others.

e. *Props and costume*

  i. Any prop choice should be essential to the persona or may end up being distracting. For example, if the persona uses a pipe during a specific fragment, then work with the pipe in rehearsal so that the prop seems clearly part of the persona. If the prop feels like it is getting in the way after much rehearsal, drop it as it may become more of a distraction to the audience.

  ii. Be careful of going "prop crazy" with too many objects. Again, the audience may be distracted by *the performer using the props rather than engaging the persona.*

  iii. The same applies for costume. Do not worry about elaborate costuming. The embodiment of the persona relies upon solid internal and external performance choices, not on "the right costume."

      iv. On the other hand, do not be oblivious to costuming. Wearing your Marilyn Mason t-shirt in performance may or may not be the best choice.

      v. Costume choices should work with rather than detract from the performance.

  f. As always, *purposefulness and clarity* of performance choices in staging will establish dialogical performance.

  g. Resist the urge to do something on stage because it would be "interesting" or "shocking" rather than motivated by the text. In this case, the audience would be paying attention to the shock value rather than dialogically engaging the persona in the autoethnography; it is spectacle without purpose rather than story, display rather than embodiment. Remember ethical pitfalls.

5. *Use of Time*

  a. Remember in the discussion of form in chapter 3, a performative autoethnography is usually constructed in fragments and is seldom chronological. Let the performance reflect these differences and fissures in the use of time.

  b. A scene that occurs in the recent or distant past can be presented through flashback.

  c. The performer might choose to embody self or other at an earlier age.

  d. The persona can move back and forth through time commenting on what was going through her mind during a particular incident or conversation.

  e. Changes or transitions from one time frame to the next can be believably indicated by a 1–2 second freeze in between. As always, if the performer is committed to the performance choice, the audience will willingly accept the convention.

6. *Familiarity with Text*

    a. Memorization of the performance is preferable; in my classes it is mandatory. Holding a script disrupts embodied performance choices and hampers an audience's dialogical engagement with the performance.

    b. Nervousness and performance apprehension is completely normal and expected. The best way to address nervousness is rehearsal: prep, prep, and more prep.

    c. Always remember that the audience will not know you have made a mistake or dropped a line unless you indicate it in performance.

    d. *Focus and concentration: Focus and concentration on performance choices and commitment to the performance process are absolutely essential to an effectively embodied performance.* The level to which you are committed to, and believe in, the performance is directly related to the level to which the audience dialogically engages. Whatever an audience feels about the content of the performance, if you believe in the performance, they will as well, and then generate their own meanings and interpretations.

        i. This means that upon taking stage, one NEVER stops the performance or breaks out of persona (unless this is a conscious and purposeful choice in the text).

        ii. Always concentrate and remain focused while in performance, especially when—and this will happen—you forget a line. No matter how much I rehearse, I always forget a line at some point in performance. Stay calm, stay in persona, ad lib until the line comes to you.

        iii. Always remember that the audience will never know that you have dropped a line unless you indicate as much.

Audience

After all performance choices have been made and rehearsed, remember that the goal is dialogical performance with the audience. Our hope is rather than commenting upon how "good" the performance was, that audience members will comment upon the ways in which the performance caused them to generate meaning about issues in their own lives through a "generative autobiography" (Alexander 2000) as discussed earlier. Dialogical performance creates reflection, conversation, and change personally and politically. When I perform "Call It Swing," I'm hoping that a white audience member might critically recall their own "white moment," or regardless of skin color, an audience member might think critically about their own relationship with their father, or their own parenting strategies when educating about race and class. When the "articulate body" (Pineau 2000) is engaged in critical reflection, writing, and performance, the audience is invited into their own lives and into the lives of others to collaborate in dialogue.

It is time now to merge the interdependent parts of the textualizing body. The critically reflective body, the words on the page, and the performing body on stage, like the dialogical performance process, will change, challenge, and embrace one another as they move through the process together. Zeb Scanlan's performance of "Tats" changed dramatically when he took the page onto the stage, or in other words, when he began analyzing the text for internal elements to embody through voice, body, and space in performance choices. Meggie Mapes's autoethnographic text of "Yet To Name" was transformed when she began speaking and moving this very embodied experience in rehearsal.

Performative autoethnography depends upon the deep communication between body, paper, and stage to realize its critical potential in engaging audiences to generate meaning in their own lives. This is why we do performative autoethnography.

Performance wants your body.
She loves your body
Constructs your body.
She is the substance between the word and the body.
She suffers no fools.
Demands respect
Accepts mistakes
Absorbs your own excess.

If she takes you as her lover
go to her
give yourself to her
body and soul.
She will expect nothing less.
But know that she has many lovers.

She will weep with you at the unfaithfulness of words
leave you speechless at the imperialism of words,
and she will be there
when they fail you
helping you eat them up
and spit them out.

If you come to her with body broken, empty, fruitless,
She will take you in her arms
and with pen in hand
help you construct
another
body-language-body-language.

Warm-ups for Embodying Performative Autoethnography

> *The wonderful paradox in the ethnographic moment*
> *of dialogue and Otherness is that communion with the*
> *Other brings the self more fully into being and, in doing so,*
> *opens you to know the Other more fully.*

D. Soyini Madison, *Critical Ethnography,* 9

These warm-ups, as performative autoethnography itself, are designed to engage the "wonderful paradox" Madison describes. The warm-ups should be used at any point in the writing or rehearsal process; use them anytime you feel stuck in rehearsal, or cannot figure out a performance choice, or simply need some inspiration.

1. *Sculpting/embodiment*: Choose a moment in your text.

    a. Brainstorm the internal elements of that moment.

    b. Starting from the top of your head, choose a position for each part of your body that would illustrate/represent/ engage the internal elements of that moment.

    c. How is the head held? What does the neck feel like in that moment? The arms, do they feel heavy, empty, etc.?

    d. This exercise can be done in pairs and groups. One performer is the artist, the other is the clay to be sculpted.

        i. The exercise is non-verbal so that the artist can concentrate on reflecting the internal elements externally in the sculpture.

        ii. Any touching of the "clay" occurs gently and only on the joints of the body.

    e. How might this translate into performances choices?

2. *Movement/embodiment*: Spend 5–15 minutes moving as the persona.

    a. Try not to speak words during this exercise so as to concentrate fully on the movement of the body, arms, legs, guts, etc.

    b. Walk around, sit, stand.

    c. As you begin to feel more comfortable, choose specific fragments or moments in the text; then move seeking to embody the *specific internal elements* of the moment.

3. *Voice/embodiment*: gradually begin to add voice to the body work in exercise 2. Remember to let the voice be motivated by the specific internal elements.

4. *Mask/metaphor/embodiment*: Make a mask that symbolizes the complexity of your performative-I persona.

    a. The form of the mask should symbolize metaphors in the text. Consider, for example, "Katrina" in the opening of chapter 3. What symbols might be on that mask?

    b. Consider how the metaphoric conceptualizations of *ethical pitfalls* may figure into the mask.

    c. Consider using the mask in certain parts of the performance as a prop, or as a symbol described by the persona.

    d. *Self-other interaction*: using the above directions, create a mask of someone in the text.

5. *Narrate the mask*: After creating masks as in exercise 4, explain the mask to a group either in class and/or outside of class. Be open to how this may change parts of the text by making certain fragments more specific, or by adding or subtracting fragments.

6. *Ethics*:

    a. Make a mask representing each of the ethical pitfalls as they may relate to your persona or someone else.

b. Choose one of the ethical pitfalls in chapter 3 and embody part of the text as that unethical stance. Reflect upon how this felt in rehearsal. This will expand your ideas and performative dimensions of ethical performances choices.

Chapter Six

Body, Paper, Stage

and Back Again

The performance is over. You realized that you were capable of much more than you thought, much more doing and knowing and being. It is cliché at this point to say that the journey has just begun, but at the insistence of my students, I must say it. The last assignment in the performative autoethnography class is for groups of students to identify themes across their performances, and then to create a collage of their group members' scripts.

Within this performance, almost to a person, students express the desire to start "at the beginning" with what they know now. It is, of course, due to the textualizing body, the process of body and text and performance moving in, around, and with one another until they *are* each other, already advising and rewriting your engagement with self/other/body/culture. And so this will continue outside of the classroom where it becomes an everyday critical pedagogy of hope and transformation. It becomes a practice of vulnerably engaging the collisions and communions with others as we seek to find ways of living that allow for a diversity of being, a multiplicity of stories. It is the creativity, critique, and cultural engagement needed for success in our personal and professional lives.

Students also report that the process of performative autoethnography changed how they relate to their body in the world, their engagement with others, and their perceptions of difference. It is not that one "likes" one's body more, but that through performative autoethnography one is engaged with the color, size, cultural being of one's body as it is constructed in various contexts. It is that he may perhaps feel more authorial control over how he "writes" and "performs" his body and when and where and why.

And it is not that she now "gets along" with others better because of performative autoethnography, but that she may perhaps be a bit more ready to engage the complexities of being and doing with others. She understands that there are many stories housed in those with whom she relates, stories that she may or may not agree with or understand. She is not as uncomfortable with the inchoate.

It is not that he now "understands" other cultures, but rather that he sees culture as fluid, in flux, moving in and around bodies and behaviors and being. He sees how culture is (re)written on himself and others. He sees perhaps that the boundaries between cultural differences are constructed by larger systems of power to divide people and conquer, to quell energizing curiosity of difference with numbing fear and ignorance.

Performative autoethnography is seldom easy, but it is always possible, and hopefully, pedagogical. When I feel the possibilities "inside me, in my chest, in my lungs and throat" (Gale and Wyatt 2008, 795), then I know, paradoxically, that I am in that liminal space, that I am onto/into something besides my own individual singular body. I know I am in a place possible for the *doing* of knowledge with others where "the stories that emerge in each case rise up against the norms that deny their integrity" (Pollock 1999, 12). Hope resides in unruly bodies, articulate bodies, bodies performing theory from the edges and failures of coherency, heterogeneity, and autonomy.

Words are imperfect, unfaithful, imperialistic, break bones. But they're all we've got. When conceptualizing loss in a post-9/11 critical imagination of hope, "keeping our hands on performance and our eyes on theory" (Madison 2006, 245), we might raise our heads from the ashes, our faces covered with the dust of souls, our empty arms embracing the furious absence, and then, filling it with the possibility of healing through an engaged and critical life.

There is nothing for it but to do it.

A Final Thought as We Move Forward in a Textualized Body

When I read/write scholarship,

I want to *feel* scholarship.

I want it to seep into the skin of the reader, of the hearer,
    of the knower,

Melt into her bones,

Move through her blood

until the words become transformed

Through her own genome

Her own body,

Her own life and recognition of self

Where she then looks into her own/other-made mirror

        looking back and forth through time,

"each one of our ancestors on our tongues" as Elizabeth
    Alexander has said,

then passionately, articulately,

crafts   something

some scholarship,

some episteme,

some epiphany

that seeps into my skin,

into my bones,

into my blood
where borders bleed as Conquergood says
where differences are connective tissues
and the lines between our bodies
and our lands
become traversable.

I want to be personally and political entangled
by scholarship.
I want it to take away my sight and help me find it.
I want it to break my bones and help me mend them.
I want it to stop my heart
    so it might pound in a rhythm with others'.
I want it to make my empty arms ache
    for an embrace.

Other-wise,
what
is the
autoethnographic
point?

References

Adichi, Chimamanda. The Danger of a Single Story. TEDGlobal 2009. Filmed July, 2009, posted October 2009. http://www.ted.com/talks/chimamanda_adichie_the_danger_of_a_single_story.html.

Albright, Ann Cooper. Dancing Bodies and the Stories They Tell. *Choreographing Difference: The Body and Identity in Contemporary Dance.* Lebanon, NH: University of New England Press, 1997.

Alexander, Bryant. *Skin Flint (or, The Garbage Man's Kid):* A Generative Autobiographical Performance Based on Tami Spry's *Tattoo Stories. Text and Performance Quarterly* 20, 1, 2000. 97–114.

———. *Performing Black Masculinity: Race, Culture, and Queer Identity.* Walnut Creek, CA: AltaMira, 2006.

Alexander, Elizabeth. Inaugural Poem. Performed at the inauguration of President Barak Obama, Washington D.C., 2009.

Anzuldua, Gloria. *Making Face, Making Soul/Haciendo Caras: Creative and Critical Perspectives by Feminists of Color*. San Francisco: Aunt Lute Books, 1995.

———. *Borderlands/La Frontera, The New Mestiza 3rd Ed*. San Francisco: Aunt Lute Books, 2007.

Bacon, Wallace. *The Art of Interpretation 3rd Ed*. New York: Holt, Rinehart, and Winston, 1979.

Behar, Ruth. *The Vulnerable Observer: Anthropology that Breaks Your Heart*. Boston: Beacon, 1997.

Bell, Elizabeth. *Theories of Performance*. Thousand Oaks, CA: Sage, 2008.

Bhabha, Homi. *The Location of Culture*. New York: Routledge, 1993.

Bochner, Arthur P., and Carolyn Ellis, eds. *Ethnographically Speaking: Autoethnography, Literature, and Aesthetics*. Walnut Creek, CA: AltaMira, 2002.

Bowman, Ruth. "Keynote Presentation." St. Cloud State University Performance Festival, St. Cloud State University, St. Cloud, MN, 2005.

Burke, Kenneth. *On Symbols and Society*. Ed. Joseph Gusfield. Chicago: University of Chicago Press, 1989.

Butler, Judith. *Excitable Speech: A Politics of the Performative*. New York: Routledge, 1997.

———. *Gender Trouble: Feminism and the Subversion of Identity*. New York: Routledge, 1999.

———. *Giving an Account of Oneself*. New York: Fordham University Press, 2005.

Capecci, John and Timothy Cage. *Living Proof: Telling Your Story to Make a Difference*. forthcoming.

Clifford, James and George Marcus. *Writing Culture: The Poetics and Politics of Ethnography.* Berkeley: University of California Press, 1986.

Conquergood, Dwight. Performing as a Moral Act: Ethical Dimensions of the Ethnography of Performance. *Literature in Performance* 5: 1985. 1–13.

———. Rethinking Ethnography: Towards a Critical Cultural Politics. *Communication Monographs,* 58: 1991. 179–194.

———. Beyond the Text: Toward a Performative Cultural Politics. *The Future of Performance Studies: Visions and Revisions.* Ed. Sharon Dailey. Annandale, VA: NCA, 1998. 25–36.

———. Performance Studies: Interventions and Radical Research. *The Performance Studies Reader.* Ed. Henry Bial. New York: Routledge, 2004. 311–322.

Crawford, Lyall. Personal Ethnography. *Communication Monographs,* 63, 2, 1996. 158–70.

Davis, Miles. "The Miles Davis Story" Dir. Mike Dibbs. IMDbPro. TV Documentary, 2001.

Deleuze, Gilles and Felix Guattari. *A Thousand Plateaus: Capitalism and Schizophrenia.* Minneapolis: University of Minnesota Press, 2009.

Denzin, Norman K. *Performance Ethnography: Critical Pedagogy and the Politics of Culture.* Thousand Oaks, CA: Sage, 2003.

———. Analytic Autoethnography, or De`ja` Vu All Over Again. Eds. Scott A Hunt and Natalia Ruiz Junco. *Journal of Contemporary Ethnography* vol. 35, no. 4, 2006a.

———. Politics and Ethics of Performance Pedagogy: Toward a Pedagogy of Hope. *The SAGE Handbook of Performance Studies.* Eds. D. Soyini Madison and Judith Hamera. Thousand Oaks, CA: Sage, 2006b.

Denzin, Norman K. and Michael D. Giardina. Introduction: Ethical Futures in Qualitative Research. *Ethical Futures in Qualitative Research*. Walnut Creek, CA: Left Coast, 2007. 9–39.

Denzin, Norman K., Yvonna Lincoln and Linda Tuhiwai Smith, eds. *Handbook of Critical and Indigenous Methodologies*. Thousand Oaks, CA: Sage, 2008.

Dickinson, Emily. "Because I could not stop for Death." *The American Tradition in Literature 5ᵗʰ Ed.* Eds. Bradley, Beatty, Long, and Perkins. New York: Random House, 1981.

Dolan, Jill. *Geographies of Learning: Theories and Practice, Activism and Performance*. Middletown, CT: Wesleyan University Press, 2001.

Ellis, Carolyn. *The Ethnographic I: A Methodological Novel about Autoethnography*. Walnut Creek, CA: AltaMira, 2003.

———. Relational Ethics. *Ethical Futures in Qualitative Research*. Eds. Norman K. Denzin and Michael Giardina. Walnut Creek, CA: Left Coast, 2007.

———. *Revision: Autoethnographic Reflections on Life and Work*. Walnut Creek, CA: Left Coast, 2009.

Ellis, Carolyn and Arthur Bochner. *Composing Ethnography: Alternative Forms of Qualitative Writing*. Walnut Creek, CA: AltaMira, 1996.

Ellis, Carolyn and A. P. Bochner. Analyzing analytic autoethnography: An autopsy. *Journal of Contemporary Ethnography, 35,* 2006. 429–449.

Fabian, Johannes. *Time and the Other: How Anthropology Makes its Objects*. New York: Columbia University Press, 1983.

———. *Anthropology with an Attitude*. Stanford, CA: Stanford University Press, 2001.

Fenske, Mindy. The Aesthetic of the Unfinished: Ethics and Performance. *Text and Performance Quarterly*, 24,1, 2004. 1–19.

Freire, Paulo. *Pedagogy of the Oppressed.* New York: Continuum, 1970.

Gale, Ken and Jonathan Wyatt. *Becoming Men, Becoming-Men? A Collective Biography. International Review of Qualitative Research,* 1, 2, 2008.

———. *Between the Two: A Nomadic Inquiry into Collaborative Writing and Subjectivity.* Newcastle upon Tyne, UK: Cambridge Scholars Publishing, 2009.

Gerrtz, Clifford. *The Interpretations of Cultures.* New York: Basic Books, 1973.

Gingrich-Philbrook, Craig. "Bite Your Tongue: Four Songs of Body And Language," *The Green Window: Proceedings of the Giant City Conference on Performative Writing.* Eds. Ronald J. Pelias and Lynn C. Miller. Carbondale, IL: Southern Illinois University Press, 2001. 1–7.

———. Autoethnography's Family Values: Easy Access to Compulsory Experiences. *Text and Performance Quarterly* Vol. 25, No. 4, 2005. 297–314.

Gomez-Pena, Guillermo. *Danger Border Crossers.* New York: Routledge, 2000.

Goodall, H.L. *Writing the New Ethnography.* Walnut Creek, CA: AltaMira, 2000.

———. *Writing Qualitative Inquiry: Self, Stories, and Academic Life.* Walnut Creek, CA: Left Coast, 2008.

Grande, Sandy. Red Pedagogy: The Un-Methodology. *Handbook of Critical and Indigenous Methodologies.* Eds. Norman K. Denzin, Yvonna Lincoln and Linda Tuhiwai Smith. Thousand Oaks, CA: Sage, 2008.

Hamera, Judith. Performance Studies, Pedagogy, and Bodies in/

as the Classroom. *Teaching Performance Studies.* Eds. Nathan Stucky and Cynthia Wimmer. Carbondale, IL: Southern Illinois University Press, 2002. 121–130.

———, ed. *Opening Acts: Performance in/as Communication and Cultural Studies.* Thousand Oaks, CA: Sage, 2006a.

———. Performance, Performativity, and Cultural Poesies in Practices of Everyday Life. *The SAGE Handbook of Performance Studies.* Eds. D. Soyini Madison and Judith Hamera. Thousand Oaks, CA: Sage, 2006b. 46–64.

hooks, bell. *Teaching to Transgress: Education as the Practice of Freedom.* New York: Routledge, 1994.

———. *Remembered Rapture: The Writer at Work.* New York: Henry Holt & Co., 1999.

Iyer, V. (2004). Exploding the Narrative in Jazz Improvisation. *Uptown Conversation: The New Jazz Studies.* Eds. R. O'Meally, B. H. Edwards, and F. J. Griffin. New York: Columbia University Press. 393–403.

Jackson, Alecia Y. and Lisa A. Mazzei. Experience and "I" in Autoethnography: A Deconstruction. *International Review of Qualitative Research*, 1, 3, 2008. 299–317.

Jackson, Michael. *Minima Ethnographica: Intersubjectivity and the Anthropological Project.* Chicago: University of Chicago Press, 1998.

Jago, Barbara J. Postcards, Ghosts, and Fathers: Revising Family Stories. *Qualitative Inquiry*, 2, 4, 1996. 495–516.

Jones, Joni. Teaching in the Borderlands. *Teaching Performance Studies.* Eds. Nathan Stucky and Cynthia Wimmer. Carbondale, IL: Southern Illinois University Press, 2002.

Jones, Stacy Holman. Autoethnography: Making the Personal

Political. *The Handbook of Qualitative Research*. Thousand Oaks, CA: Sage, 2005.

———. Autoethnography is Queer. *The Handbook of Critical and Indigenous Methodologies*. Thousand Oaks, CA: Sage, 2008.

Kaplan, Caren. Resisting Autobiography: Outlaw Genres and Transnational Feminist Subjects. *Women, Autobiography, Theory: A Reader*. Eds. Sidonie Smith and Juila Watson. Madison: University of Wisconsin Press, 1998.

Kingsolver, Barbara. *Small Wonder: Essays*. New York: Perennial, 2002.

Krieger, Murray. *Words about Words about Words: Theory, Criticism, and the Literary Text*. Baltimore: Johns Hopkins University Press, 1992. 6, 15.

Lakoff, George and Mark Johnson. *Metaphors We Live By*. Chicago: University of Chicago Press, 1980.

LaMott, Anne. *Bird by Bird: Some Instructions on Writing and Life*, New York: Anchor Books, 1995.

Lance, Wallace. Multicultural Critical Theory. At Business School? *New York Times*, January 10, 2010. section BU, 1.

Langellier, Kristin M. and Eric Peterson. *Storytelling in Daily Life: Performing Narrative*. Philadelphia: Temple University Press, 2004.

Liakos, Antonis. Canonical and Anticonanical Histories. *Ethnographic Moralia: Experiments in Interpretive Anthropology*. Eds. Neni Panourgia and George Marcus. New York: Fordham University Press, 2008.

Long, Beverly Whitaker and Mary Frances HopKins. *Performing Literature: An Introduction*. Upper Saddle River, NJ: Prentice-Hall, 1982.

Madison, D. Soyini. *Critical Ethnography: Method, Ethics, and*

Performance. Thousand Oaks, CA: Sage, 2005.

———. Performing Theory/Embodied Writing. *Opening Acts: Performance in/as Communication and Cultural Studies.* Thousand Oaks, CA: Sage, 2006.

———. Dangerous Ethnography. *Qualitative Inquiry and Social Justice.* Walnut Creek, CA: Left Coast, 2009.

Madison, D. Soyini and Judith Hamera, eds. *The Sage Handbook of Performance Studies.* Thousand Oaks, CA: Sage, 2005.

Mapes, Meggie. Yet To Name. unpublished autoethnography, 2010.

Marcus, George E. Contemporary Fieldwork Aesthetics in Art and Anthropology: Experiments in Collaboration and Intervention. *Ethnographic Moralia: Experiments in Interpretive Anthropology.* Eds. Neni Panourgia and George Marcus. New York: Fordham University Press, 2008.

Marsalis, Wynton with Selwyn Seyfu Hinds. *To a Young Jazz Musician: Letters from the Road.* New York: Random House, 2005.

Max, D.T. The Unfinished. *The New Yorker*, March 9, 2009.

McLaren, Peter. *Teaching against Global Capitalism and the New Imperialism: A Critical Pedagogy.* Lanham, MD: Rowman & Littlefield Publishers, 2004.

Muncey, Tessa. *Creating Autoethnographies.* Thousand Oaks, CA: Sage, 2010.

Mutua-Kombo, Eddah. Their Words, Actions, and Meaning: A Researcher's Reflection on Rwandan Women's Experience of Genocide *Qualitative Inquiry*, 15, 2009. 308–323.

Paley, Grace. Debts. *Enormous Changes at the Last Minute.* New York: Farrar, Straus and Giroux, 1974.

Panourgia, Neni and George Marcus. *Ethnogrpahic Moralia: Experiments in Interpretive Anthropology.* New York: Fordham University Press, 2008.

Papagaroufali, Eleni. Carnal Hermeneutics: From "Concepts" and "Circles" to "Dispositions" and "Suspense". *Ethnographic Moralia: Experiments in Interpretive Anthropology.* Eds. Neni Panourgia and George Marcus. New York: Fordham University Press, 2008.

Pelias, Ronald. *Performance Studies: The Interpretation of Aesthetic Texts.* Dubuque, IA: Kendall Hunt, 1999.

———. *A Methodology of the Heart : Evoking Academic and Daily Life.* Walnut Creek, CA: AltaMira, 2004.

———. Performative Writing: The Ethics of Representation in Form and Body. *Ethical Futures in Qualitative Research.* Eds. Norman K. Denzin and Michael Giardina. Walnut Creek, CA: Left Coast, 2007.

Pelias, Ronald J, and Tracy Stephenson Shaffer. *Performance Studies: The Interpretation of Aesthetic Texts.* Dubuque, IA: Kendall Hunt, 2007.

Pendergast, Monica. Poem is What? Poetic Inquiry in Qualitative Social Science Research. *International Review of Qualitative Research* 1, 4, 2009.

Pineau, Elyse Lamm. Nursing Mother and Articulating Absence. *Text and Performance Quarterly* 20, 1, 2000. 1–19.

———. Critical Performance Pedagogy: Fleshing Out the Politics of Liberatory Education. *Teaching Performance Studies.* Eds. Nathan Stucky and Cynthia Wimmer. Carbondale, IL: Southern Illinois University Press, 2002.

Pollock, Della. Performing Writing. *The Ends of Performance.* New York: New York University Press, 1998. 73–103.

———. *Telling Bodies Performing Birth.* New York: Columbia University Press, 1999.

Poulos, Chris. *Accidental Ethnography: An Inquiry into Family Secrecy.* Walnut Creek, CA: Left Coast, 2009.

Richardson, Laurel and Elizabeth Adams St. Pierre. Writing: A Method of Inquiry. *The Handbook of Qualitative Research.* Eds. Norman K. Denzin and Yvonne Lincoln. Thousand Oaks, CA: Sage, 2005.

Roloff, Leland. *The Perception and Evocation of Literature.* New York: Scott Foresman & Co., 1973.

Russell, Larry. A Long Way toward Compassion. *Text and Performance Quarterly,* 24, 3 and 4, 2004. 233–254.

Scanlan, Zebadiah. Tats. From "Through the Earlobe." Director Chris Collins. Performed at St. Cloud State University, MN, April 2010.

Schechner, Richard. *Between Theatre and Anthropology.* Philadelphia: University of Pennsylvania Press, 1985.

Sher, Gail. *One Continuous Mistake: Four Noble Truths for Writers.* New York: Penguin, 1999.

Smith, Linda Tuhiwai. *Decolonizing Methodologies: Research and Indigenous Peoples.* New York: St. Martin's Press, 1999.

Smith, Sidonie. Performativity, Autobiographical Practice, Resistance. *Women, Autobiography, Theory: A Reader.* Eds. Sidonie Smith and Julia Watson. Madison: University of Wisconsin Press, 1998. 108–115.

Spry, Tami. Performative Autobiography: Presence and Privacy. *The Future of Performance Studies: Visions and Revisions.* Ed. Sheron Dailey. Annandale, VA: National Communication Association Publication, 1998. 254–259.

———. Performing Autoethnography: An Embodied Methodological Praxis. *Qualitative Inquiry* 7, 2001a. 706–732.

———. From Goldilocks to Dreadlocks: Racializing Bodies, *The Green Window: Proceedings of the Giant City Conference on Performative Writing.* Eds. Ronald J. Pelias and Lynn C. Miller. Carbondale, IL: Southern Illinois University Press, 2001b.

———. Illustrated woman : Autoperformance in "Skins : A Daughter's (Re)construction of Cancer" and "Tattoo Stories : A Postscript to 'Skins.'" *Voices Made Flesh: Performing Women's Autobiography.*Eds. Lynn C. Miller, Jacqueline Taylor and M. Heather Carver. Madison: University of Wisconsin Press, 2003.

———. Paper and Skin: Bodies of Loss and Life. An autoethnography performed in various venues across the country, 2004.

———. A Performance-I Copresence: Embodying the Ethnographic Turn in Performance and the Performative Turn in Ethnography. *Text and Performance Quarterly,* 26, 4, 2006. 339–346.

———. Systems of Silence: Word/less Fragments of Race in Autoethnography. *International Review of Qualitative Research,* 1,1, 2008. 75–80.

———. Bodies of/and Evidence. *International Review of Qualitative Research* 1, 4, 2009. 603–610.

———. Call It Swing: A Jazz Blues Autoethnography. *Cultural Studies<->Critical Methodologies* 10, 4, 2010a. 271–282.

———. Performative Autoethnography: Critical Embodiments and Possibilities. *SAGE Handbook of Qualitative Research.* Thousand Oaks, CA: Sage, 2010b.

Starnino, Carmine. Five From Ireland. *Poetry,* November, 2008. 149–161.

Strine, Mary Susan. Mapping the 'Cultural Turn' in Performance Studies. *The Future of Performance Studies: Visions and Revisions.* Ed. Sharon Dailey. Annandale, VA: NCA, 1998. 3–9.

Stucky, Nathan. Fieldwork in the Performance Studies Classroom: Learning objectives and the Activist Curriculum. *The SAGE Handbook of Performance Studies.* Eds. D. Soyini Madison and Judith Hamera. Thousand Oaks, CA: Sage, 2006. 261–277.

Stucky, Nathan and Cynthia Wimmer, eds. *Teaching Performance Studies,* Carbondale, IL: Southern Illinois Press, 2002.

Trinh, T. Minh-ha. *Woman, Native, Other.* Bloomington: Indiana University Press, 1989.

——. *When the Moon Waxes Red.* New York: Routledge, 1991.

Turner, Victor. *The Anthropology of Performance.* New York: PAJ Publications, 1986.

Worthen, W.B., Disciplines of the Text: Sites of Performance. *The Performance Studies Reader 2nd Ed.* Ed. Henry Bial. New York: Routledge, 2008.

Young, Vershawn Ashanti. *Not Your Average Nigga: Performing Race, Literacy, and Masculinity.* Detroit: Wayne State University Press, 2007.

Index

About the Author

Tami Spry is a Professor of Performance Studies in the Communication Studies Department at St. Cloud State University (SCSU) in Minnesota. She employs autoethnographic writing and performance as a critical method of inquiry into culture and communication, teaching courses in beginning and advanced performative autoethnography, performance of literature, and collaborative writing in performance. Dr. Spry's performance work, publications, directing, and pedagogy focus on the development of cultural critique that engenders dialogue about difficult sociocultural issues; specifically, her work engages issues of race, sexual assault, grief, shamanism, and mental illness. Dr. Spry has presented performance research across the country and abroad, most recently in the UK at the University of Bristol, the University of Cambridge, and the University of Oxford.

Dr. Spry was the director of the Players Performance Group at SCSU, facilitating student's original productions, and directed international performance studies conferences at SCSU focusing on autoethnography, masculinity, and immigrant issues. She also teaches abroad in Alnwick, England, and has conducted ethnographic work in Chile with Mapuche and Peruvian shaman on the performative dimensions of healing rituals.

She received the Central States Communication Association Award for Outstanding Scholar in Performance Studies for 2010. Dr. Spry's publications appear in *Text and Performance Quarterly, Critical Studies* ↪ *Critical Methodologies, Qualitative Inquiry, International Review of Qualitative Research, Women and Language,* the *SAGE Handbook of Qualitative Research,* and various anthologies. Her latest performance, Call It Swing, performed at the Sixth International Congress of Qualitative Inquiry at the University of Illinois, Urbana, embodies jazz as a critical method of inquiry.

Tami lives in the country with her husband Barry, three cats and a dog, and is an avid perennial gardener; they are proud of their dear son Zeb, who currently studies abroad and is a writer and performer.